HOW TO RECOGNISE

MACHINE LACES

Pat Earnshaw

Gorse Publications

British Library Cataloguing-in-Publication Data

A catalogue record for this book is available from the British Library

ISBN 0 9524113 2 6

© Pat Earnshaw 1995

Printed by Butler and Tanner, Frome, Somerset

Typeset by Alastair Thompson, Paris, France

for Gorse Publications, P O Box 214,
Shamley Green, Guildford GU5 0SW,
England

By the same author:

> The Identification of Lace
> A Dictionary of Lace
> Bobbin and Needle Laces, Identification & Care
> Lace in Fashion, from the 16th to the 20th centuries
> Lace Machines and Machines Laces, Vol I
> Needle-made Laces
> Youghal and other Irish Laces
> Youghal Lace the Craft and the Cream
> Threads of Lace from Source to Sink
> Embroidery Skills: Needlelace
> Outlines and Stitches: Halas needlelaces
> Limerick Run Laces
> Embroidered Machine Nets: Limerick and Worldwide

Cover illustration: draft for a Madras lace. (Courtesy: Morton Young and Borland, Newmilns, Ayrshire, Scotland).

CONTENTS

Note: a fairly strong magnifier or loupe may be needed, at first, to spot the machine lace features.

TERMS

The vocabularies of hand and machine laces overlap and are often confusing.

BOBBIN AND SPOOL: alternative terms for an implement on which threads can be wound.
Bobbins are the wood or bone sticks used in bobbin laces, one to hold each thread. They may number 8 to 1,000.
Bobbins (sometimes called *brasses*) are the thin circular discs holding one of the sets of threads of Twist-net machines. They are supported in metal carriages and commonly number between 2,000 and 3,000.
Bobbins or *spools* are the thread holders on Barmen machines.
They stand vertically and number about 64.
Spools hold the patterning yarns in the Lace Curtain machine.
Bobbin-lace and *bobbin-made* imply hand laces; *Bobbinet* is made by machine.

GROUND is the structured openwork of a lace. It forms a background to the design, holding the parts together and giving them stability. It may form a continuous meshwork, or a series of bars.

The **OUTLINE** of design elements may be called:
Gimp the (usually) thicker thread inserted around the motifs of a bobbin lace as it is made.
Gimp an alternative name for the clothing, clothwork or solid areas of a Leavers or Lace Curtain design when produced by beam or spool threads.
Liner a thicker thread run in, or attached to the surface by embroidery, or incorporated in the fabric, in machine laces.
Contour or *outline thread/foundation cord* The thread, couched down to the pattern, which fixes the outline of each part of the design in needle laces, delineating the shape which is then filled in with stitches.
Cordonnet a cord, or stitch-covered padding, attached over the contour thread of a needle lace, giving it a three-dimensional appearance.

PILLARS In the Barmen machine, straight or near-straight vertical threads which support the active spool threads as they interweave around them.
In warp-knitting machines (the Warp Frame and Raschel), the vertical lines of knitted loops, on either the face or reverse of the lace, one pillar per warp end.

PILLARING A means of carrying the pattern threads forward from one motif to another without forming floats. They are wrapped around the vertical ground threads.

ORIENTATION Laces are frequently drafted and worn at right angles to their position during manufacture - exceptions are the deep flounces made crosswise (widthwise) of the machine.

CONTINUOUS-THREAD bobbin laces: the threads pass in continuity from the solid design areas into the ground and back again, traversing eventually the entire width of the lace.

NON-CONTINUOUS THREAD bobbin laces: the threads of the solid areas turn inwards as they reach the border of each motif, so that the design elements are separate from each other. They are then linked by the attachment of other threads which create a mesh- or bar-ground. Fresh threads are similarly joined to the motifs to construct the decorative fillings.

MACHINE NAMES
Raschel a version of the old Warp Frame, developed in 1859 and considerably modified between 1950 and the present day.
Old Loughborough and *Circular,* obsolete names for the *Bobbinet* or *Plain net* machine which produces traversed nets, with diagonally running threads.
Bobbinet and *Twist-net* are also generic terms for the group of machines including Bobbinet, Pusher, Leavers and Lace Curtain.
Barmen Beginning life as the *Dentellière,* the machine is also known in general as the *Lace Braiding Machine, Métier à Dentelle aux Fuseaux Mécaniques, Kloppelspitzenmaschine, Macchine per Pizzo Tombolo* or, more specifically, as the *Krenzler, Reising* or *Alvergnas.*

CROSS-TWIST SEQUENCE
Clothstitch CTC (rarely TCT, reversed clothstitch)
Halfstitch CT
Wholestitch CTCT (rarely TCTC, reversed wholestitch).

1

HISTORY AND THE MACHINES

Introduction

By the mid-18th century laces had already been made by hand for several centuries, and had been high fashion since the 1550s.

The incentive to copy these laces by a mechanical process was a by-product of the Industrial Revolution which, beginning in England in the early 18th century, had already addressed itself with some success to the development of machines that could spin and weave.

In the 1760s the only other machines which could in any way produce openworks were the ancient Stocking Frames. Invented over 150 years before, they had busily churned out wool, silk and occasionally cotton hosiery ever since. Their openwork was quite minimal, achieved only by a tedious hand-manipulation of the stitches.

Stocking Frames were compact stolid structures made of slabs of wood. They resembled an open crate which held not only a seat for the knitter, but all the needles, ticklers, presses and other pieces needed to produce successive rows.

By the mid-18th century hand-made laces were moving, in England, into a slow decline. For state occasions Flemish laces such as Mechlin, Brussels and Valenciennes, and French laces such as Argentan, Alençon and blonde, were favoured.

Even in France fashion was favouring the exuberant Lyons silks, while the pale laces, inconspicuous against them, were exploring a trend towards simplicity, their broad designs reduced to tiny repetitive sprigs, their fine mesh grounds absorbing progressively larger areas of the available space. Tightly gathered into robings and ruffles, their skilful and time-consuming work was all too easily replaced by gauze puffs or muslin frills.

This doldrum of hand-lace production, sinking ever more deeply into lethargy as the century drew to its close, left a gap which some novelty such as a totally new form of lace might hope to fill.

Apart from the intense curiosity and passion for experiment which had characterised the Industrial Revolution from its inception, the irresistible carrot which lured the inventors on must have been the prospect of an invasion of the immensely profitable market which hand-made laces had monopolised for so long - for hand laces, like machine, were from their very beginning a commercial venture.

Two contemporary models suggested themselves as prototypes for the very first machine laces: the superfine openwork hand-knitting then being imported from Spain, and the highly valued and expensive bobbin-made net, produced in Flanders and Devon, and known as droschel.

This net had first appeared at the end of the 17th century and its popularity continued through the 18th. It formed at first the background for richly patterned laces known as point d'Angleterre but, as the trend towards simplicity gathered momentum, it reached an extreme point where there was no design for it to attach itself to and it was made totally plain, in a series of narrow strips barely .25 inches wide, joined lengthwise by a laborious hooking process

Single press point net

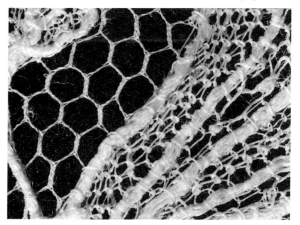

Droschel forming the background of a needle lace, mid-18th century

Further desperate efforts by more inventors led, in the 1780s, to a fast (no-run) 'double pressed point net'. Though it produced little effect upon the fashion scene before 1800, its lower cost, novelty value and undoubted beauty led to its ultimate popularity and acceptance even by royalty - the Princess Charlotte selecting it, in 1817, for her wedding gown.

which rendered the seams almost invisible, and in linen yarn so fine as to be almost weightless.

Soon a whole mob of inventors - in harmony or in cut-throat competition - were seeking feverishly to copy it, by a knitting process.

Within a decade a 'single press point net' of lustrous silk, its hexagonal meshes a mere one millimetre across, came off the machine, its ephemeral lightness rivalling that of droschel itself. Unfortunately it was indeed ephemeral, the slightest snag or yarn breakage causing a rapid unravelling, the silk loops slipping easily through each other until only a mess of tangled threads remained. This tendency could be slowed, even prevented, by a special 'finishing' process which was developed by the French, who had lost no time in pirating one of the machines.

Double press point net with tambour embroidery

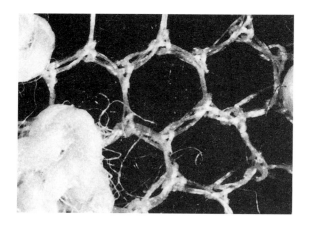

The Warp Frame

Knitting on the Stocking Frame was similar to hand knitting, that is the thread was stretched horizontally across the needles, in a weft direction.

In the 1780s a more extensive modification of the Stocking Frame was undertaken. Separate spools of thread, one for each needle, were placed at the top of the Frame and it was along these that the knitting proceeded. Vertical pillars of loops were produced, cross-connected at intervals to hold them together.

This new machine was the Warp Frame.

Its first products were solid fabrics which could be cut without risk of unravelling. But soon, in competition with the point nets, the loops were spaced apart, creating an openwork.

Left: a Stocking Frame machine. The knitter sits on the bench with his arms outstretched to reach the extremes of the knitting area.

Below: Warp Frame lace. Both the solid areas and the open ground are vertically knitted.

The Bobbinet

The Bobbinet machine (Courtesy: Heathcoat, Tiverton, 1980)

In 1808 came another invention, this time of a totally different character. Instead of expensive silk yarn it used cotton, and instead of imitating the knitting technique, it used the twisting and crossing techniques of the halfstitch ground of Bucks point and Lille laces.

Unlike the Stocking Frame which used only a single thread stretched horizontally, and the Warp Frame which used a single set of multiple threads stretched vertically, this new machine - which became known as the Bobbinet - used two distinct sets: vertically-arranged warp ends which passed from a roller below to another roller above where the net could accumulate, and bobbin threads held on thin circular spools which were equal in number to the warps.

The bobbins were propelled rapidly and unceasingly along narrow slots (combs) passing between the back and front of the machine, through the gaps of the strung warp ends. Each swing was known as a motion, and 140 of them could be packed into every minute.

In the split second following each motion, the warps shifted a little to the right or left, thus placing themselves first on one side then on the other of the bobbin threads, creating the impression that they were twisting around them.

This process imitated, perhaps as closely as could ever be possible, the technique of hand-made bobbin laces. In these the threads are worked in pairs which can number anything from 4 to 500 depending on the type of lace to be produced. At any one time they can be distinguished into two sets, the vertically-lying passives and the diagonally

Left: clothstitch. Right: halfstitch. The course of the workers is marked with arrows. The other threads are passives.

The two thread movements of bobbin laces, which are imitated by the Bobbinet.

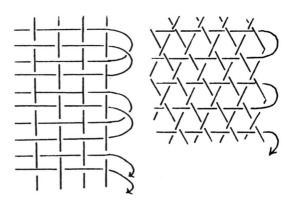

TWIST Z

CROSS S

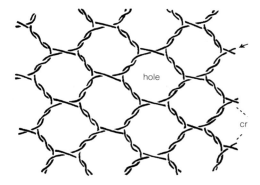

Two-twist bobbinet

Four-twist bobbinet

progressing workers, the sets interacting with each other in a crossing and twisting manner. Passives and workers are interchangeable, and additional threads can from time to time be added in or threads no longer wanted taken away. The solid design areas are worked in either clothstitch or halfstitch, while the openwork ground, like the decorative filling stitches, can take many varied forms.

In the Bobbinet machine on the other hand the distinction between the two sets of threads is quite unalterable. While the warps shunt constantly through small distances in a widthwise direction, the bobbins without interrupting the velocity of their swings are shifted one slot sideways on every twelfth motion, setting them on a long gyratory journey from left to right along the front comb bar and right to left along the back comb bar, the complete circuit requiring, on a wide machine, over 5,000 motions during which the net progresses upwards some considerable distance, and the bobbins make a diagonal passage across the entire width of the net. It is this progression which produces the crosses at the top and bottom of each mesh. The process is called traversing, and the product a traversed net.

Apart from its far greater width, bobbinet is indistinguishable from its prototype.

Coming, like the weft- and warp-knitted nets of the modified Stocking Frames, quite plain off the machines, the only copies of patterned hand-made laces that were possible over the next two or three decades were by hand embroidery, using run, chain-stitch or appliqué techniques.

In both the knitting and bobbinet machines, the intention to deceive was quite obviously there from the very beginning, in the shape of the meshes, in the embroidered patterning, and finally in the automated Jacquard system applied to the machines

from the late 1820s onwards. The problem even today of distinguishing machine laces from similar forms made by hand is a measure of their supreme success.

The popularity of bobbinet provided an incentive for a continuing development of the machine, referred to at that time as the Old Loughborough. While the original 2-twist or round net later developed the more expensive variations - 3- and 4-twist square or diamond nets - greater diversifications were on the way. Only four years later, prototype Pusher and Leavers machines had evolved, and in 1846 came the third major Twist-net development, the Nottingham Lace Curtain machine.

The economy and durability of their laces had, by 1819, driven the weft-knitted nets out of the English market, but they survived for at least two decades longer in France from where, crisply finished, they returned to a warm welcome from English buyers.

The warp-knitted nets had greater adaptability and potential. They were soon patterned on the machine and, overcoming many vicissitudes, have emerged in recent years as the electronically controlled Raschel derivatives which now occupy a dominating position in - indeed are threatening to monopolise - the machine lace market. Their early patterning was automated first by Dawson's wheel (a cam cut to allow repetitive loop movements) then, from the late 1820s, by the Jacquard, enabling them to simulate with great charm the black silk bobbin laces of Chantilly, which were reaching their peak of popularity during the 1860s. The vertical knitted pillars, exposed on the surface of the cloth, were interconnected at variable intervals to form elaborate and extensive designs.

The Pusher

A Pusher machine, manufactured in 1860 and still active in Lyons in 1993. It works in a tilted position. The harness cords above link the Jacquard head in the roof to the pushers which motivate the carriages (Courtesy: Goutarel, Lyons).

Of the three Bobbinet developments, only the Pusher retained the traversing of bobbin threads which had characterised their progenitor. Its Jacquard-automated patterning, developed in the late 1830s, selected certain bobbins in every row, prodding them into action by metal pushers - from which the machine derived its name - to create areas of clothing or solid design within the net ground.

A single pusher. On the right the cut end of its harness cord. On the left the thread-holding brass bobbin encased in a steel carriage, upon which it acts (Goutarel).

The diagonal movements of the bobbin threads. 1-3 solid areas of imitation halfstitch. 4-6 traversed net. X: lack of activity by the pushers causes the bobbin threads to twist around the warps, forming holes (diagram: Bette Stijnman).

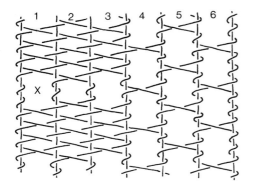

The diagonal passage of the bobbin threads continued through these design areas, producing an effect of hand-made halfstitch. The straight threads cutting across the diagonal bobbin pathway were the warps, but whereas in the Pusher laces the straight threads lay lengthwise, in hand-made laces they passed widthwise.

The Pusher's rather cumbersome patterning process rendered it slow and at a disadvantage in comparison with the Leavers, but its finest copies of the silk Chantilly and Spanish blonde laces were magnificent.

The thread (liner) used to outline the pattern areas, could not be added during manufacture and had always to be added after the lace had been taken off the machine. It could be run in by hand, or attached as a cord to the surface using a single-needle hand-operated embroidery machine.

Though picots could be added to straight edges while the lace was still on the machine, shaped pieces required the later hand-addition of ready-made borders, thus adding considerably to the time and cost of production.

Above: a fan leaf of Pusher lace c1890.

Below: Pusher lace with cord liner attached to the surface.

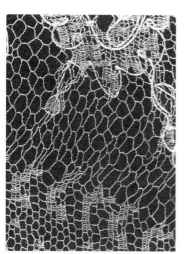

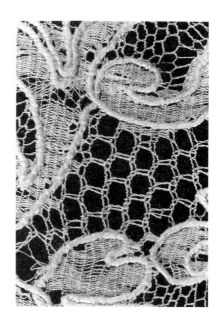

Left: Pusher lace with hand-run liner above, no liner below. The craquele net is made of coffin-shaped meshes; the spots by isolated patches of halfstitch.

A Leavers machine. The numerous beams lie below, the lace accumulates above. The Jacquard apparatus lies further to the right (Courtesy: Birkin, Nottingham).

In the Leavers traversing was abandoned. All the yarns lay vertically, capable only of limited right-left movements, resulting in more rigid 'straight-down' laces.

It introduced more threads, doubling the warps into front (right or S-twist) and back (left or reverse-twist) sets, and adding a whole new batch of rollers - up to 400 - which supplied additional patterning yarns known as beams or gimps. These were motivated by a sophisticated system of independently moving guide bars.

In this way, in time, every type of marketable bobbin lace was successfully attempted including Binche, Honiton, Antwerp, Valenciennes, Bucks point, Maltese, Spanish blonde, Mechlin, Lille, Milanese and Brussels, as well as craft laces such as Teneriffe - even Leavers broderie anglaise was registered at the Public Records Office, Kew, between 1876 and 1882.

The beams were needed only in the pattern areas. In the ground they spiralled around the vertical strands, a process known as pillaring.

For fifty years from the time of the Jacquard application, in the late 1830s, the Leavers was supreme. Its success depended not only on the more restricted movements of a vastly increased number of threads, but on its development of a variety of techniques, of which the most important were Independent Beam, Bobbin Fining and Centre Gimp, though there were many hybrids.

INDEPENDENT BEAM: the warps were omitted and the number of beams increased. The presence of only two sets of threads, bobbin and beam, gave the laces a clarity of aspect which was deceptive. In particular quite wide areas, identical in appearance to the clothstitch of bobbin laces, could be produced.

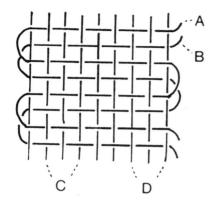

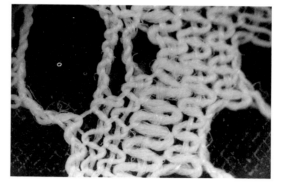

Left: Independent technique, analysis of the threads in the solid areas. In the lace they would continue for short throws on either side to bind the motifs to the surrounding areas. A = back gimp. B = front gimp. C = bobbin. D = sleepers (middle gimp).

Right: Bobbin fining. The bobbin threads twist around two warps on either side of a central sleeper.

BOBBIN FINING: here the beams were omitted, leaving only bobbins and warps. This reduction in thread number, combined with the use of fine silks, natural or artificial, could produce light shiny fabrics, often effectively copying bobbin designs. As in other Twist-net laces the warp threads shogged to right and left of straight bobbin yarns, but strong weighting pulled the warps downwards so that in the finished lace they lay straight while the bobbin threads, lightly sprung, spiralled around three at a time, the central warp lying passive, as a 'sleeper'. The result was a zigzag effect, impossible to confuse with either the halfstitch or clothstitch of bobbin laces.

CENTRE GIMP: all three sets of threads were used. In consequence, pillaring had to occur in the ground areas to dispose of the surplus patterning yarns, and sometimes the ground had to continue through the design. This feature easily distinguishes them from bobbin laces, but they can still be confused with embroidered nets in which an uninterrupted meshwork is decorated by hand or machine embroidery.

Leavers machines were able to add both picots (1827) and liners (1847) during manufacture, but this feature is not necesarily a help in dating, since hand finishing - for prestige or convenience - continued for a number of years and some, such as the hand-cutting of complex scallops, even to the present day.

Centre gimp. The net passes right through the design areas. Arranged as made.

The Lace Curtain machine

Above: detail of a Lace Curtain machine, showing some of the top board spools, and the Jacquard harness passing upwards to the roof (Courtesy: Morton, Young & Borland, Newmilns, Ayrshire).

Below: A Lace Curtain lace with lighter and denser areas of clothing, and Swiss net. Note the bobbin ties. Arranged as made.

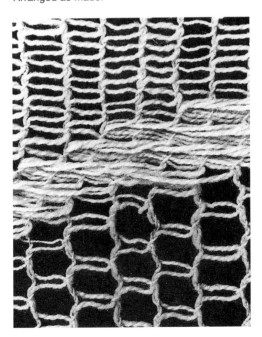

The warp and bobbin threads occupied similar positions to those of other Twist-net machines, the warps strung vertically while the bobbins swung back and forth between them.

As in the Leavers there was no traversing, and the threads ran 'straight-down'. Also like the Leavers the Lace Curtain machine had additional patterning threads, but wound on spools not rollers, and divided into two sets known as Top Board and Bottom Board spools. There were separate spools for every thread in every repeat and the overall total in a large machine might top 7,000.

The Jacquard arrangement was similar to the Pusher. The apparatus and cards were lifted into the roof, from where they manipulated the yarns by remote control, using a series of spreading strings known as the harness and intermediaries (jacks) which acted on the spool threads.

The machine's chief market lay not in fashion but in soft furnishings such as curtains, bed- and table-covers, and its imitations were almost entirely limited to the hand-knotted filet with its run-stitch and darned designs. It seldom used either picots or liners.

One of its most distinctive features was the 'bobbin ties': the bobbin threads appear to spiral down the warps and tie the patterning (spool) threads to them.

The Barmen

The Barmen machine was developed originally in France and shortly afterwards in Germany in the town from which it takes its name. Although it worked by the twisting together of threads to produce imitations of bobbin lace designs and techniques, it is not included in the Twist-net category since it makes no net, and has no division into warp and bobbin yarns. It had a quite different origin, evolving in the second half of the 19th century from the Braiding machine, by the introduction into its solid fabrics of an increasing amount of openwork.

Unlike the Pusher, Leavers and Lace Curtain machines, with their enormous working widths of up to 420 inches, the Barmen was very small, no more than about 4ft in diameter - being limited in size by its circular shape, since the workman setting it up had to have arms long enough to reach the centre.

The Barmen's construction also restricted its imitations to bobbin laces of fairly simple form such as torchon, and to a maximum width of 8 inches.

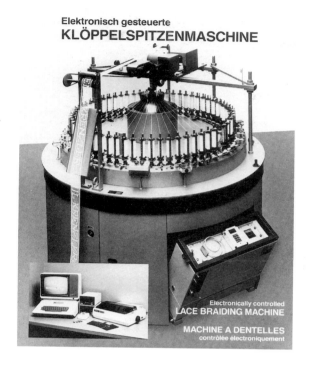

Elektronisch gesteuerte
KLÖPPELSPITZENMASCHINE

Electronically controlled
LACE BRAIDING MACHINE

MACHINE A DENTELLES
contrôlée electroniquement

Right: an electronically controlled Hacoba Lace-Braiding [Barmen] Machine, Model SKZ 7-E, system Krenzler. Threads from the circle of spools converge on the central mandrel. The lace has been worked with the name of the machine, Krenzler (Courtesy: Hacoba, Wuppertal).

Below: a 2-thread Barmen lace of synthetic horsehair. The solid areas are of diagonal clothstitch.

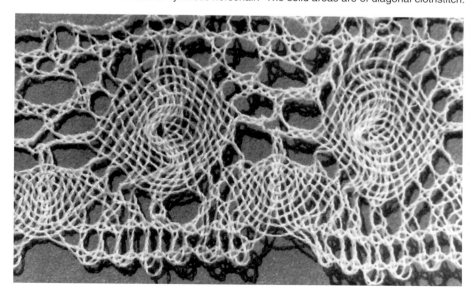

The spools or bobbins which held the threads arose vertically around the circumference of an upper table. By Jacquard action they were moved selectively along controlled pathways, imitating with supreme exactitude the twists and crosses made by a human lacemaker. The result was that the thread paths traversed the lace from side to side, they were easy to follow, there was no excess of threads to be disposed of in the non-patterning areas, and no pillaring in the ground.

In contrast to bobbin laces however there was no distinction into vertical passives and diagonally interacting workers: all the Barmen spools were at appropriate times equally capable of activity in a manner which cannot in detail be compared with the constant change in function from workers to passives and passives to workers characteristic of bobbin laces.

The threads from the spools converged on a central pinnacle known as the mandrel, and from this the lace rose up in a hollow column instead of lying flat, as it would on a lacemaker's pillow, a difference in arrangement which led to problems when the machine attempted to copy clothstitch and halfstitch. Its general preponderance of diagonal movements meant that the natural direction of the straight lines of the halfstitch areas was lengthwise of the lace rather than widthwise, and a diagonal clothstitch was more easily produced than a plain-weave. These features are easily recognised.

However the best Barmen laces could - with a greater expenditure of time and money - copy the real 'plain-weave' forms. They are then some of the most difficult machine imitations to recognise with certainty.

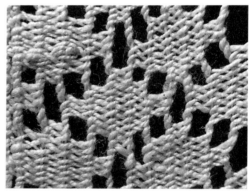

Top right: a 1-thread Barmen lace and three 2-thread laces. All of ramie (*Lace and Embroidery Review*, 1912).

Middle right: diagonal clothstitch supported over inactive pillar threads with double pillar threads in the footing.

Below: Halfstitch. Left, bobbin lace. Right, Barmen lace.

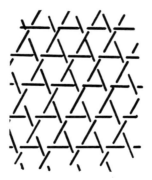
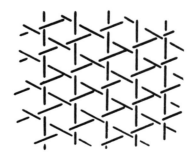

Above: Saurer 3040 Pentacut machine. To the left the electronic control system (Courtesy: Saurer, Arbon, Switzerland).
Below: the basic detached buttonhole stitch of needle laces.

All the machines mentioned so far, whether Knitting or Twist-net, concentrated their efforts on copying bobbin laces. A further group, developed during the 1860s to 1880s, was able in addition to copy craft laces, embroidered laces such as cutwork and filet and, very effectively; a whole range of needle laces both contemporary and antique.

Needle lace, as made by hand, requires a single thread and a sewing needle, and the construction of a series of semi-circular loops interlocking with each other row after row. Needle laces were in fact a derivative of embroidery, with the background fabric omitted and the stitches secured only by passing through each other.

It was natural therefore that needle laces should be copied by embroidery machines. The two most important were the Handmachine and the Schiffli, both developed primarily in Switzerland.

The HANDMACHINE had a horizontal bar of needles, each threaded with a short length of yarn through a central eye. The bar was made to advance and retreat by foot-operated pedals, pushing the needles repeatedly back and forth through fabric stretched taut on a rectangular frame.

The positioning of the stitches depended not on the needle movements, which were constant and unvarying, but on the up-down left-right gliding of the frame itself, movements controlled by an operative through a system of levers described as a pantograph.

The machine's needle-movements, passing entirely through the fabric and back again, produced stitches which resembled so closely those of hand embroidery that its products, as with Leavers Independent and Barmen laces, are very difficult to identify. It can give an excellent effect of darning, and so simulate the clothstitch of bobbin laces. While it cannot imitate true knots, it can give a fair

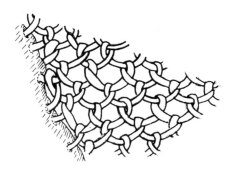

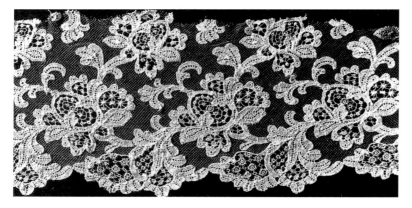

Left: Handmachine embroidery on two-twist bobbinet.

Below: detail of Handmachine chemical lace guipure. Note darned effect.

impression of them by making short stitches repeatedly over the same area. It can give a reasonably good, though on close inspection not totally convincing, impression of blanket stitch, along a scalloped border for example.

It cannot entirely recreate the semi-circular looping (or detached buttonhole stitching) of genuine needle laces, but its products were sometimes embellished by hand in a manner intentionally calculated to enhance the similitude. Because of its set-up, its patterning was restricted to a series of fairly short repeats and it could not, economically, manage large all-over designs which would require only a small number of needles and, ultimately, be cheaper by hand. The needles, being attached to a bar, operated in unison, making

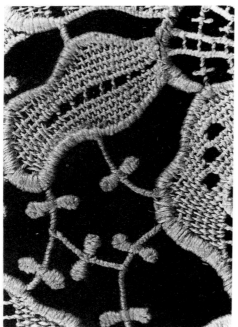

identical movements, and since every needle was responsible for a complete repeat, all the repeats were of necessity identical, the threads being carried from one part to another in a totally similar manner - something that would be not only unlikely but completely pointless in an embroidery worked by hand.

The Handmachine could copy mesh-ground bobbin or needle laces simply by working its embroidery on net. In guipure laces, where instead of a meshwork the design motifs were linked by bars, imitation required a more elaborate technique: the embroidery was worked on a fabric scheduled for destruction, leaving nothing finally but a series of interlocking stitches conveying almost uncannily the impression of a hand-made lace. At first, the degrading of the background fabric was carried out by a chemical process, often relying on some form of corrosion and the products were in consequence referred to as chemical or burnt laces. They were also known as Swiss laces (since the technique was developed and very extensively used in Switzerland) or simply guipures (a general term for all hand or machine laces where the parts of the design are held together by bars instead of by meshes). The last full-size commercially active Handmachine ceased production in 1986 when its Swiss operative retired at the age of 99.

The SCHIFFLI machine, developed a little later, had an immediate advantage over the Handmachine in that it could, from the start, make use of external power such as steam and electricity. Schiffli embroideries were therefore more speedily produced, and since in manufacturing the time taken is always directly proportional to the cost of production, its copies of hand-made laces though not cheap - for the machine was delicate and easily upset - were soon less expensive than those of the Twist-net machines and often, at least from a distance, more convincing.

Left: Schiffli emboridery on net, subsequently cut away in parts by hand.

Below: Schiffli chemical lace guipure.

On closer inspection however the similarity fell apart. The Schiffli worked not with a single set of threads of limited length as did the Handmachine, but with two sets of continuous threads, one held in a series of horizontally placed needles fed from small reels, the other, on the far side of the fabric, held in an equal number of closed boat-shaped spools from which the name schiffli (Swiss German for a small boat) was derived. The two sets interacted at the fabric surface, in the manner of a domestic sewing machine, to produce a lockstitch. Their yarns often differed slightly in count or colour, so that an examination of the face and reverse sides of the lace will reveal the technique used.

Also, there is no way that a tightly compacted set of lockstitches can be mistaken for either hand-stitching or the thread manipulations of bobbin- and needle-lacemakers. Indeed the general effect of fuzziness is, with experience, quite unmistakable, yet the designs were copied with such extreme exactitude that it is all too easy, at a quick glance, to be misled. Even the Schiffli's simulated darning may require close inspection for its falsity to be recognised.

One easily recognisable feature is the substitution of cotton for linen yarn in copies of antique hand-made laces.

The frame movements which resulted in patterning were at first controlled by a pantograph similar to that used on the Handmachine. By the mid-1890s the Schiffli, now known as the Automat, had the labour-saving Jacquard applied to it, and the operative formerly needed to maintain the stitch by stitch movements of the pantograph could be dispensed with.

Like the Handmachine, the Schiffli could produce copies of either mesh-ground or guipure laces, by embroidering on net or onto a chemically degradable fabric. Its catalogue of copies included nearly all 19th-century and many earlier needle and bobbin laces such as reticella, punto in aria, Venetian gros point and coralline, reseau Venise, point de gaze, Alençon, Argentan, Honiton, Duchesse, Rosaline, Milanese, the popular tape laces (laces of pre-made tapes) which began in the middle of the 19th century, and the raised Irish crochets so fashionable in Paris in the early 1900s.

Above: a design for a bobbin lace fan leaf by J.Hrdlicka, Vienna.

Below: a design for a Schiffli embroidery by Paul Rudolf, Plauen, c1907.

The disadvantage of machine laces, from the point of view of high society and haute couture, was that they were cheap, and therefore available to millions of women who had not previously been able to afford them. In the past, lace had been the prerogative of the Court, and although during the 18th century and particularly in England the wearing of lace became a hallmark of the nouveaux riches, in the rapidly expanding and already differentiating middle classes the further effusion of lace-wearing to people who were not even middle-middle class seemed rather outrageous. Indeed the visibly obvious discriminatory factor of lace versus no lace was no longer valid, and the need to assert, unmistakably, a social superiority was from time to time transformed into a vicious denigration of the imitations as common, vulgar, white, derivative, in poor taste - in short the kind of stuff no lady would be seen in, dead or alive.

For a long time this ploy was not as successful as it might have been, firstly because of the extreme similarity of design and even of texture between hand and machine laces; secondly because by the mid-19th century machine-spun cotton yarn far surpassed the contemporary linen both in fineness and strength; and thirdly because machine laces were, by the 1850s to 70s, achieving a standard of excellence that few of the hand laces of that period could match, while the details of the copies were so meticulous that only by the extreme incivility of approaching their noses so closely towards the lace that they almost wiped against it could the curious ladies discover the truth of its origin and perhaps, maliciously, disclose a pretension.

Not until the Arts and Crafts and the Art Nouveau Movements of 1870-1910 did machine laces finally wean themselves from dependence on the inspiration of the hand-made. The long search for a closer and closer approximation to the traditional became pointless as hand laces themselves threw off the old image and ventured into dynamic and original designs.

The new concept of Lace as Art was more cautiously embraced by machine manufacturers to whom, unavoidably, the commercial aspect remained a prime consideration. But, prompted by academics and Schools of Design, many beautiful and innovative styles appeared.

However this swing of emphasis did little to ease the problems of distinguishing hand from machine laces and the technical criteria of recognition continued to apply.

Lace and the Wage Factor: the Raschel

The 20th-century rise in wages was destructive of the finest quality machine laces just as much as of hand. At the new wage level it was simply not commercially possible to spend sufficient time to perfect the end-product. The hand-drawing of designs and drafts, the hand-punching of the Jacquard cards, threading, repairs and finishing all occupied an enormous number of hours and consumed a huge outlay of capital, which it became increasingly difficult to recoup.

Only an increase in speed of production could counteract the increase in cost, and for hand-lacemakers and the older machines this seemed an insurmountable problem.

Both took instead the alternative pathway of sharpening the dichotomy, already in place during the 19th century, into up-market exclusivity and down-market banality.

In this form the industry survives today. While public taste controls the mass bread-and-butter machine lace productions, the limited haute couture market still demonstrates the superb skills, ingenuity, even genius of which lace machines are capable, when the money to pay for them is available.

For newer machines the option of increasing the speed of production remained open. The Warp Frame, modified and known as the Raschel from 1859, took on a new lease of life in the 1950s, under the initiative of Karl Mayer of Obertshausen, Germany. Up to that time it had, like other machines, depended on the use of either natural or man-made fibres, such as cotton and rayon but, coinciding with the machine's revivification came the first appearance on the market of the new synthetic yarns, notably nylon. Taking full advantage of their tensile strength and resistance to abrasion and, over the following decades, of the evolving electronic control of design and manufacture, Raschels attained the amazing speed of 1,500 cm of lace per hour, compared with the Pusher's 32 cm.

The modern Raschel has two main sets of threads: the warp ends, one per needle, along which the vertical knitting occurs; and the inlay yarns which replace by their horizontal weft-like movements the more laborious patterning formerly brought about by interconnections of the knitted pillars.

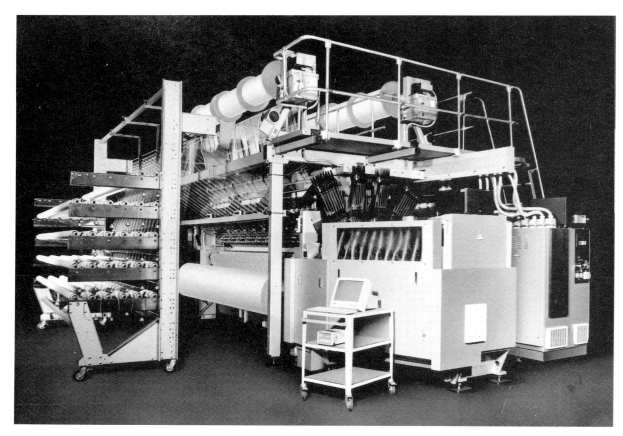

Above: The Textronic warp-knitting machine, the most highly advanced fully computerised 'Raschel', 1994. The electronic control system is shown on the right. The creel, left, holds the patterning yarns. The warps lie above the machine (Courtesy: Karl Mayer, Obertshausen).

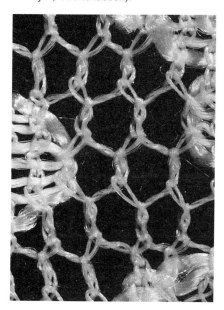

Left: reverse of warp-knitted lace showing pillars and inlay yarns.

The pillars were now placed on the reverse side of the lace with the inlay threads on the face. With hand laces no longer a serious market competitor, the Raschel concentrated on imitations of Leavers laces which still, though the quality was much diminished since their early 20th-century glory, led the market.

One by one effects, previously unique to Leavers, were added to the Raschel's repertoire - the border of picots, the incorporation of liners, the (limited) use of natural fibres, even a three-dimensional flossing effect - until today it is far from easy to distinguish Leavers laces from their warp-knitted counterpart, except by the thin and often slightly wavy pillars along its back.

Within the last few years both Schiffli and Leavers have made tentative steps into computer assisted design, and the possibilities of computer assisted manufacture are being considered.

The Madras

One further technique should be mentioned, the woven laces, or Madras. Set up like a normal if not totally modern weaving loom, their openwork depends on the gripping of the wefts by pairs of warps twisting about them in a gauze or leno-type weave. Patterning relies on heavier figuring wefts inserted across the machine in accordance with a hand-drawn draft, then cropped back mechanically to define the solid areas. The technique derives from the hand-made burattos (Italian, a sieve), constructed of silk or linen, in which the background gauze was woven on a hand-loom and the embroidery threads displayed intense and vivid colours. Madras products are also related to the loom laces of the mid-19th century, found in the peasant areas of Germany and Denmark, though in these the patterning depended not on cut wefts but on an intricate warp-manipulation.

Madras 'laces' were marketed from the mid-19th century and the Jacquard applied to the looms in the 1870s. Their designs were at first simple and sprig-like and then, following closely the fashion trends of the period, embraced in an entrancing manner the delights of the New Art and the freedom from constraint of the following non-imitative years. Many, in the late 19th century, were in muted colours.

Today, Madras is made of pure fine quality cotton, and only in Scotland.

Above: detail of cut wefts on a gauze-weave ground.

Below: Madras lace with design of poppies c1890.

2

A FACILE GUIDE TO THE RECOGNITION OF MACHINE LACES

A. *Firm indications*

Features which appear only in machine laces, so that the presence of even a single one of them can indicate beyond doubt a machine origin.

B. *Less firm indications*

Features which appear mainly in machine laces, but which also appear in some hand-made laces, or can be deliberately imitated by them.

C. *Contra indications*

Features which no machine lace can imitate, so that the presence of even a single one of them can indicate beyond doubt a hand origin.

D. *Not particularly helpful*

Features which may or may not help with recognition in any particular instance.

By using these lists, recognition should, in time, become infallible, or at least almost 100% certain.

Bear in mind however that there is a considerable range of machines and machine techniques, that hand-made laces are hugely variable even within the same category, that a single hand-lace type may be copied by several different machines or by different techniques of the same machine - and you will see that the subject is not entirely simple, and that instant recognition without adequate experience may not be easy.

A. *Firm indications*

The presence of *any* of the following indicates a machine lace. But do not expect to find *all* of them in one lace.

1. *Parallel or near-parallel lines* passing in a vertical direction through the lace, giving a ribbed effect which may be very prominent or quite weak. In the latter case the lines are more clearly visible if the lace is held up to the light. These straight lines are warp threads in the Bobbinet, Pusher, Leavers Bobbin Fining and some Lace Curtain laces; bobbin threads in Leavers Independent, and bobbin plus reverse warps in Centre Gimp. In the Warp Frame and Raschel laces the ribs may be on either the face or the reverse of the lace. They consist of knitted pillars and may be quite obvious, as part of the design, or deliberately inconspicuous.

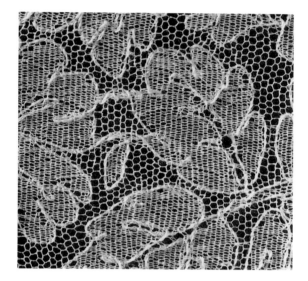

Left: vertical lines of warps in a Pusher lace.

2. *Straight down* as opposed to a diagonal progression of threads.

Below left: Leavers Centre Gimp bottom bar, with untraversed Bishops net (see p. 31). Though it looks like bobbinet, the threads pass straight down, not diagonally.

Below: Lace Curtain. The straight-down aspect is emphasized by heavy pillaring.

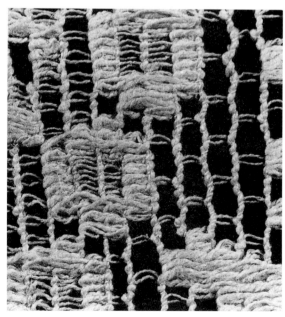

25

3. A *zigzagging* effect within the pattern areas, passing around two warps, or around three the central thread being then inactive.

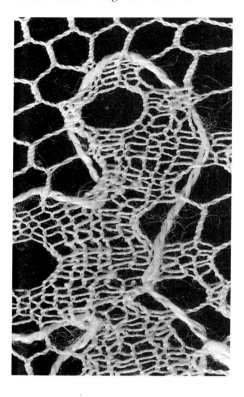

Left: Leavers zigzag fining with run-in liner.

4. *Pillaring* of the threads in the ground.

Below: cross-ground (Ariston net) in the Lace Curtain machine. A = warp. B = top board. C = bottom board. D = bobbin yarn.

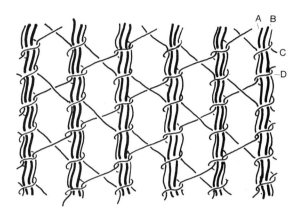

5. An *error* regularly occuring in every repeat.

Below: there are no errors in this example but the unswerving precision of the Jacquard repeat shows how any patterning error *must* recur.

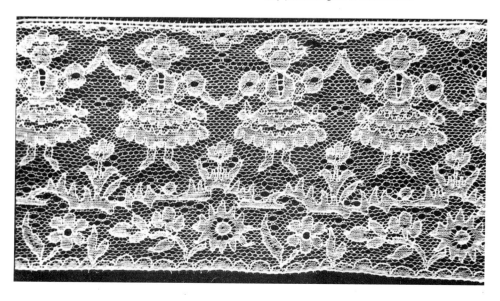

6. A *liner* with a cut on both sides (above and below) each motif.

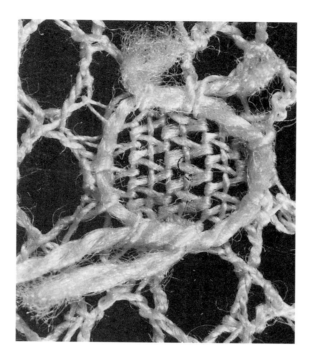

7. The use of *elastomeric yarn*. Check the lace for stretchability.

The elastomeric yarns run lengthwise of the lace. Note 'mechnical' picots.

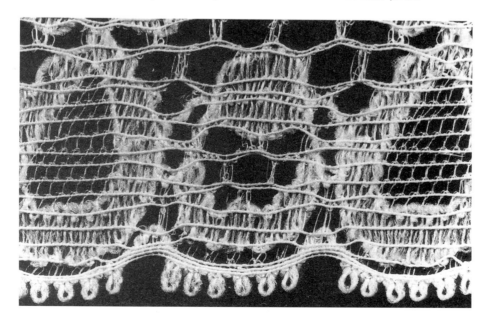

8. The twisting of the threads together is often very tight, and their *path is difficult to follow* (mainly Leavers and Lace Curtain).

The passage across the halfstitch areas appears clear, but around the edges confusion begins and continues into the cluny (raised tally), net ground and leaves.

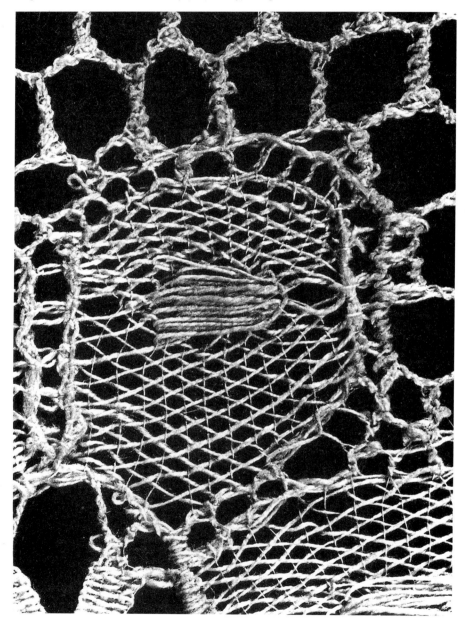

28

9. The lower border of the lace shows *cut threads* (mainly Leavers flouncing, and Lace Curtain).

Left: Leavers centre gimp flouncing in fine black silk, made crosswise of the machine, and cut above and below to separate this width from the next.

Below: Leavers bobbin fining with raised liners, the net cut away in parts, by hand, to give a guipure effect.

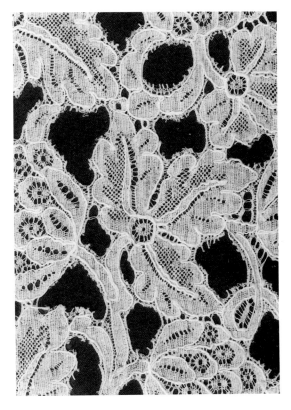

10. Pillars of *knitted loops* appear down either the face or reverse side of the lace or net. In the first case, patterning takes place by interconnecting the pillars; in the second by horizontally running inlay yarns trapped in position by the loops. Warp knitting has no handmade equivalent.

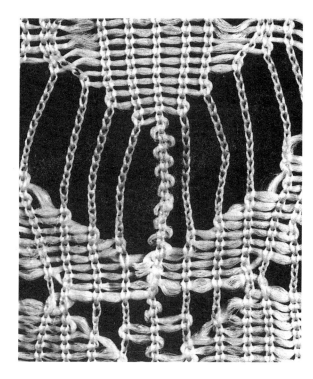

Left: warp-knitted pillars and the patterning inlay yarns, reverse side. Rayon. Raschel, 1930s.

11. *3-twist* untraversed net (no hand-made equivalent).

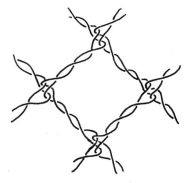

Right: 3-twist untraversed net.

12. *Square* meshes without knots (filet) or with arrowhead partitions (Swiss Net).

Below: Lace Curtain, Swiss net (left) and Filet net (right).

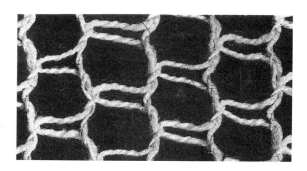

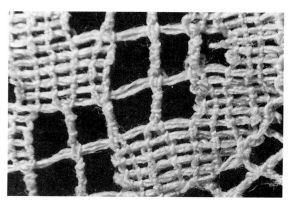

13. The presence of straight-down **Ensor net** or **Bishops net** (Leavers).

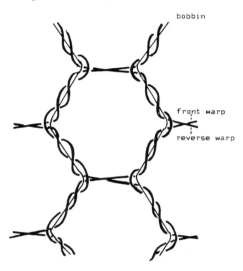

bobbin

front warp

reverse warp

14. **Lockstitch:** found in Schiffli, some Cornelys, and single-needle embroidery machines such as Singer or Adler.

Left to right, making a lockstitch.

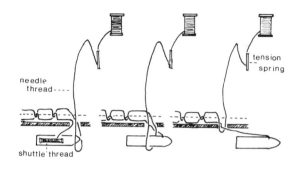

tension spring

needle thread----

shuttle thread

Bishops net has wider more consistent crosses.

15. The appearance of ***much thinner threads*** twisting among the other threads and appearing to tie them together (below left). Although bobbin laces may have thicker gimp threads, and needle laces, such as Youghal, areas of heavier and lighter density resulting in part from the use of threads of different count (below right), the general effect is in no way comparable.

Right: Youghal needle lace showing variations in thread thickness.
Below right: bobbin lace with thicker gimp thread.
Below: Leavers bobbin fining with flossing. Note passage of thin bobbin threads through the ground.

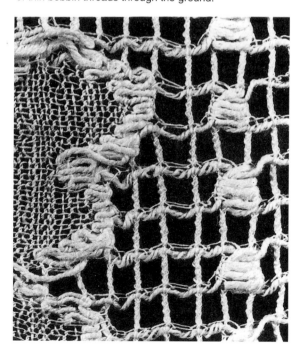

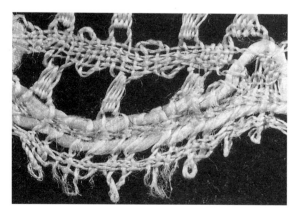

B. *Less firm indications*
A single feature is not conclusive.

1. An added, as opposed to an incorporated, *machine picot* border. Sometimes found in hand-made laces where the edges have become worn, and in embroidered nets. May be made with bobbins. Here made on the Warp Frame.

Right: a length of picots made on the Warp Frame is attached to an embroidered net.

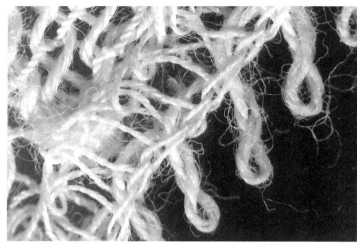

2. The *footing* (selvage) contains straight threads which, when pulled, gather the edge. In bobbin laces such pulling normally produces a diagonal puckering across the width, but if several lengthwise passives are inserted the gathering will again be in a straight line.

Left: Leavers independent, footing. The two outermost threads provide support only, and do not pass into the lace.

Below: Bobbin lace gimps showing clarity of thread passage (see no. 4. p. 33).

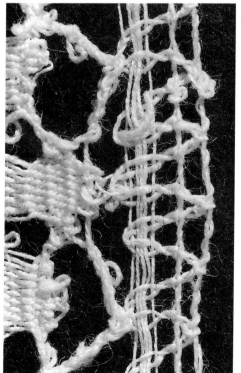

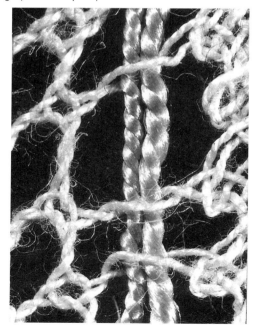

3. Short and rigidly repetitive *repeats.* This is the norm of machine-lace production, but on machines regulated by an overhead Jacquard and harness such as the Pusher, Lace Curtain, and some Raschels the design can extend across the whole length and breadth of the web, with no identical repetitions. At the same time, a fashion for short, though not 100% identical, repeat designs was characteristic of many hand-made laces from the late 18th, through much of the 19th, and into the 20th centuries.

Alençon needle lace
c1785.

4. An *inconsistent passage* of threads between design and ground. In continuous-thread bobbin laces the paired threads pass neatly over the outline thread (gimp), clasping it firmly each time. Leavers may attempt to imitate this feature, but its threads are not paired and cannot pass diagonally. The appearance can however be extremely deceptive.

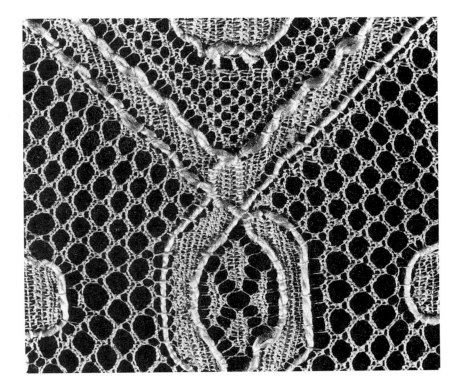

Leavers
fining.

5. *4-twist* nets can be made by hand, but only those made by machine are used for embroidery.

6. A lack of such isolated *non-repetitve errors* as might be expected from human fallibility. A danger is that the more perfect a hand lace, the greater the likelihood of its being mistaken for a machine copy.

7. The *net ground continuing through the design*. This could be an example of Leavers Centre Gimp, or an embroidered net. In appliqué laces the net continues behind, not through, the design.

Above: Schiffli embroidery on 2-twist net.

Top left: Leavers Centre Gimp.

Left: run embroidery on a 4-twist net.

8. In *'halfstitch'* areas the straight as opposed to diagonal threads run lengthwise instead of widthwise (Pusher and Barmen). Bobbin lace can imitate this (see p.16). Similarly Barmen's diagonal clothstitch can be copied by hand.

9. The *'feel'* of the lace. Machine laces are frequently stiffened with starch or gum arabic. Hand laces may also be, though to a lesser extent, and personal treatment by private hands in the past may have varied greatly, causing laces of the same type to feel sometimes stiff, sometimes limp.

10. *Cutting and rejoining* of patterned areas of lace, or *cut edges* of a net. Twist-net machines can produce either wide webs of lace or a series of vertically-arranged bands. Shaped pieces such as collars or capes, if made as such, would present a huge wastage of material which can be avoided by cutting the fabric into pre-determined parts, arranged as repeats during manufacture, and stitching them together by hand or machine. Large pieces of hand-made lace may show similar cuts and joins if they have been refashioned to make a more up-to-date accessory. Also, large pieces of bobbin lace must be made in strips and subsequently joined, for example in Chantilly and Maltese.

11. *Liners* run in or couched around the motifs, after the lace is off the machine, can pass in any direction, often aiming at a continuous passage. Where cuts occur they will be on one side only. Gimps of bobbin laces also pass in continuity and are cut on one side only, but they are clamped between the threads passing across them, and their direction is in general downwards.

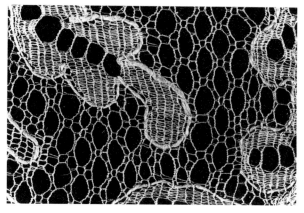

Pusher lace with cord liner attached, to pass without interruption from one motif to the next.	Leavers fining lace with run liner, also passing continuously around the motifs.

12. Difficulty in *unravelling* the lace. This applies mainly to the Lace Curtain and some Leavers machines where there is extensive pillaring. It is less noticeable in the Barmen and in the knitted-lace machines. Needle laces do not unravel easily.

13. The *width* of continuous-thread bobbin laces is limited to a few inches or centimetres, so that any really wide piece of lace or net, showing no joins, is almost certainly machine-made. The width restriction does not apply to non-continuous thread bobbin laces or to needle laces, in both of which the motifs are made separately and then joined.

C. *Contra indications*

The presence of any of these features indicates the lace is hand-made

1. Presence of interlocking semi-circular loops *(detached buttonhole stitches)*, indicating a needle lace (see p.17).

2. The presence of *knots.* No lace or embroidery machine can make a totally convincing knot, though a small net-making machine is able to construct a plain knotted filet ground which is then used for embroidery.

Hand-made fishernet knots differ in alternate rows,
the machine-made do not.

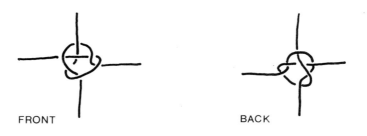

FRONT   BACK

3. The presence of *sewings* such as are used to attach ground and fillings to the solid areas of design in non-continuous thread bobbin laces.

1-6 = sewings.

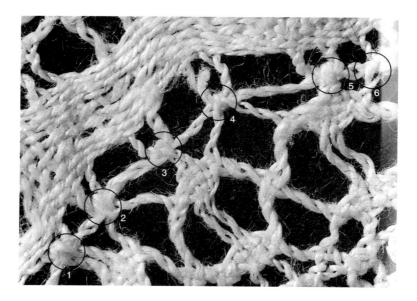

4. The presence of isolated ***non-repetitive errors***.

5. The use of fine hand-spun ***linen*** thread is never found in machine laces. But machine-spun linen is sometimes used.

6. ***Exchange bobbins*** along the footing.

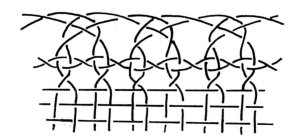

Footing of a bobbin lace. The outermost threads change from active to passive to active functions as they pass in and out of the lace.

7. ***Curvature*** of the threads to follow the shape of petals, leaves or scrolls is common in bobbin laces, and curvature of the lines of stitches in needle laces. Only the embroidery machines can imitate this. Other lace machines must work in straight lines.

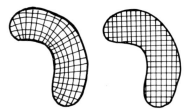

Left: hand filling-in of curved shape.

Right: machine filling-in.

8. ***Turning back*** of threads. While hand-made laces can be worked in almost any direction, lace machines can work only in one (upwards except in the Raschel where the web moves downwards). This does not apply to the embroidery machines where the frame has freedom of movement.

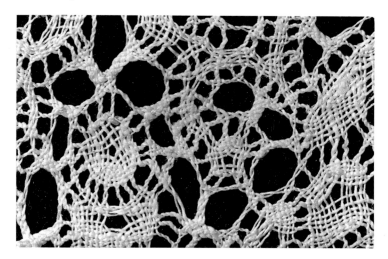

Detail of Binche lace snowflakes. Threads can enter and leave from any direction.

D. *Not particularly helpful*

1. *Reversibility*

(a) While continuous-thread bobbin laces are generally regarded as being the same on both sides, they are likely to be marginally flattened on the side next to the pricking. This is less noticeable after washing. A few bobbin laces have a cord-like gimp which rises above the surface, appearing to be separately attached though in fact it is held in the usual manner (see p. 73).

(b) Non-continuous thread bobbin laces often have additional raised work on the face side. So do many needle laces.

a   b

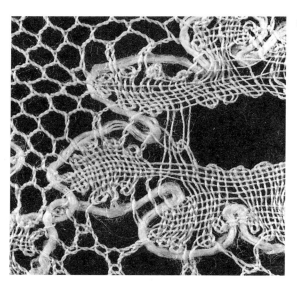 

Above: (a) continuous-thread bobbin lace with gimp.
Below: (b) non-continuous thread bobbin lace with raised work.

Top right: (b) Halas needle lace with raised outline
Below: (c) Pusher lace with run liner. Note cut above eye.

b   c

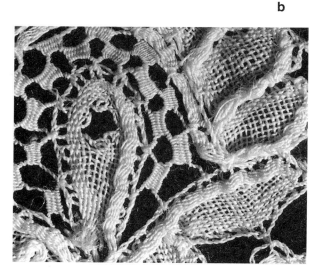 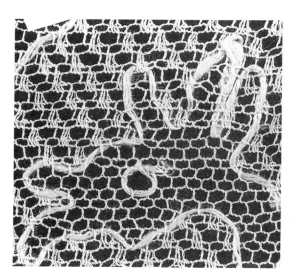

Right: (d) Barmen imitation of Scania lace showing plain-weave clothstitch.

Below left: (e) weft-knitting.
Below right: (e) warp-knitting.

Bottom left: (e) Leavers flossing.

Bottom right: (f) back-stitching on reverse side of tambour embroidery.

d

e

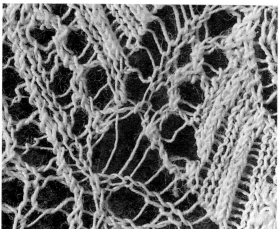

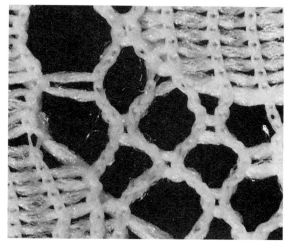

(c) Pusher laces with a run liner, or with no liner at all, are reversible.   **e**

(d) Barmen laces, and nets embroidered with run stitch, are almost wholly reversible, though cut embroidery ends are likely to be left on the reverse side.

(e) Stocking and Warp Frame laces and their derivatives, Pusher laces with a couched liner, and Leavers laces with a raised liner or flossing are not reversible.

(f) Tambour-embroidered nets have chain-stitch on the face, and back-stitch on the reverse, side.

e

f

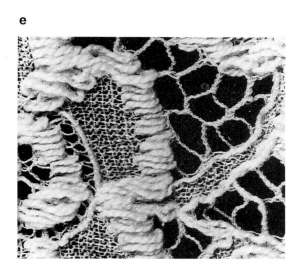

(g) The needle- and shuttle-thread configurations of the Schiffli machine, on the face and reverse respectively, are not identical (see pp. 19 and 31).

(h) In the Handmachine the carry-over of threads from one part of the embroidery to another, or from one repeat to the next, is restricted to the reverse side.

(i) Hand- or machine-appliqués have the design on one side, net on the other.

(h) Reverse of Handmachine embroidery showing cary-over of threads.

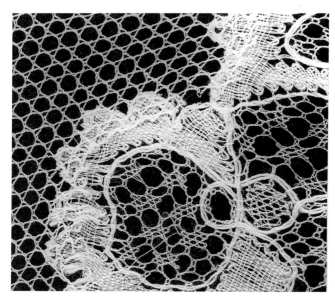

(i) Reverse of Bucks bobbin lace appliqué on machine Point de Paris net, the net cut away behind the design.

2. *Yarns*

Prior to 1803 bobbin laces were made of hand-spun linen yarn, silk, or occasionally wool. After 1803, and particularly after the early 1830s, machine-spun cotton was increasingly used. Needle laces were rarely made of cotton before the 1850s. In the 20th century hand-made laces continued to use mainly machine-spun cotton or linen.

Early knitted nets and laces used silk, or occasionally cotton. Twist-net machines used cotton from 1808, with the addition of silk from 1824. Pusher and Leavers used mainly cotton, occasionally silk or mohair. The Lace Curtain machine gave its best effects with cotton. Leavers and Barmen sometimes used machine-spun linen, and in June 1899 a patent was registered for 'Linen laces made by machinery in imitation of real hand-made laces'. In the 20th century machines turned increasingly to artificial silks, pure synthetics or polyester-cotton mixes.

3

HAND-MADE LACES AND THEIR MACHINE IMITATIONS

In Section 2 the features to look for in recognising machine laces were listed under four heads.

Now that these features are understood and can be recognised, the search can be extended to examples of hand-made laces matched with their machine imitations.

Machines imitated not only hand-made laces but also other machines, for example Leavers copied Barmen and Lace Curtain laces, and the present-day Raschel has mastered the Leavers' appearances so successfully that only the thin lines of knitted pillars on the reverse side betray it.

The geographical origin of machine laces is often hard to establish since machines work in much the same way wherever they are located.

Dating is a little easier because the start and/or finish of many techniques such as 3-twist net, bobbin fining, the attachment of picots or insertion of liners, are clearly documented.

Although the shape and size of accessories - collars, veils, jabots, plastrons - can be helpful, the machines' lesser dependence on high fashion and greater dependence on mass-marketing means that the frequent and fickle swings which are of such assistance in dating antique hand-made laces are less obviously available.

The List

ALENÇON

Above: needle lace, France, mid-19th century.
Solid areas: detached buttonhole stitch with a straight return, sometimes with an aura of picots supported over horsehair.
Decorative areas: various buttonhole stitches, often with picots.
Meshwork (see opposite).
Cordonnet: a cord closely buttonholed over (opposite, top right).
Linen or cotton.

Imitation by Pusher (below)
No buttonhole stitches, no picots, no horsehair.
All areas - solid, decorative and ground - formed by crossed and twisted threads passing diagonally.
Liner: a cord attached by machine couching (opposite, bottom right).

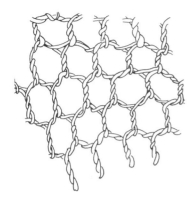

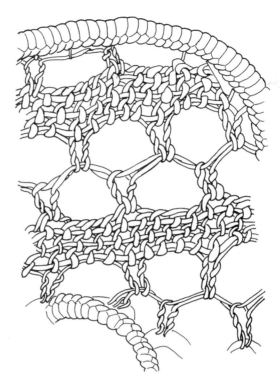

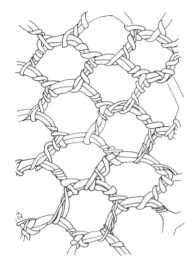

Alençon meshworks. Top: twisted buttonhole stitch with a whipped return.
Middle: the same, but the meshes twisted around with thread.
Below: horsehair supporting the picots.

Above: needle lace.

Below: Pusher.

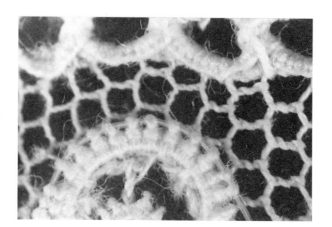

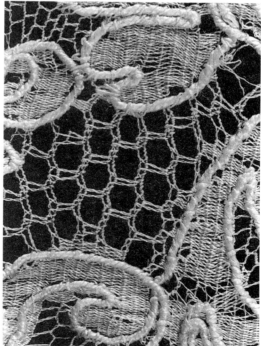

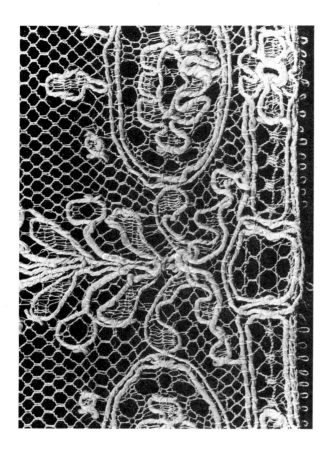

Imitation by Leavers warp fining (left)
Arranged as made.
No buttonhole stitches, no horsehair.
Solid areas: warp fining.
Meshwork: straight-down Ensor net (see p.31).
Picots: simple loops along heading.
Liner: added during manufacture, cut floats above
and below each motif.

Imitation by Schiffli embroidery on net (right)
No buttonhole stitches, horsehair or liners.
Picots may be simulated by elongated stitches.
Solid areas lockstitch, indented and polished by molten
wax. In the needle lace this effect is produced by an
aficot of steel or bone.
Meshwork: 4-twist net.

All imitations made of cotton.

44

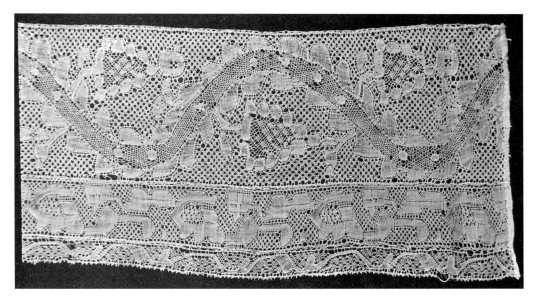

ANTWERP

Above: continuous-thread bobbin lace, Flanders/Netherlands, early 18th century, linen.
Solid areas: clothstitch.
Gimp: thin, and only in parts.
Meshwork: 5-hole ground (detail, right).
Picots: clearly continuous with inner threads.

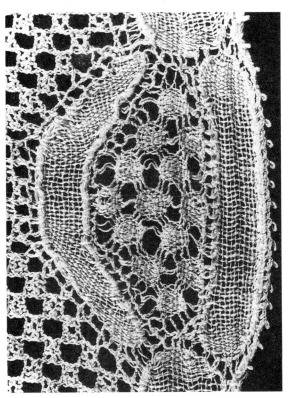

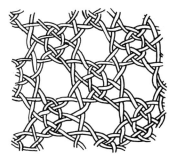

Imitation by Leavers independent (left)
Arranged as made.
Threads lie straight down, no diagonal passage. Tightly twisted together, interwoven with thin lines; their path impossible to follow except in the solid areas which simulate clothstitch. Their passage across the liner, and between the picots and the lace, irregular and unclear.

BEDS MALTESE/CLUNY/LE PUY

Above: Continuous-thread bobbin lace, England or France, c1860s. Cotton, silk or linen.

Solid areas: clothstitch with divided trails and some needleweaving effect. Threads of the arcs follow their curvature. No gimp.

Decorative areas: leaves radiating like the spokes of a wheel or arranged in long rows. Square-ended or pointed, sometimes superimposed (see below).

Ground: plaited bars which may bear picots.

Footing: exchange bobbins (see p.37).

Heading: plaited loops with small picots (9-pin border).

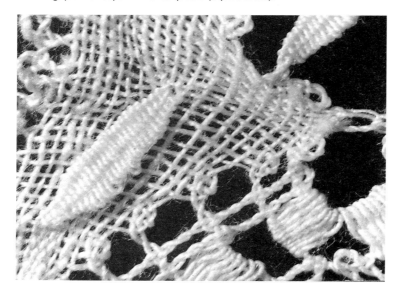

Below: bobbin lace tally and leaf

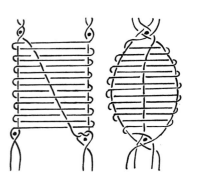

Imitation by Leavers independent (Cluny) (above)
General passage of threads straight down, apart from
widthwise beam throws. Their course difficult to follow,
especially in the spiders and raised tallies.
No diagonal passage, no curvature, no plaiting, no
exchange bobbins.

Below, detail: passage of threads through these leaves
appears untidy.
Headside picots, supported over lacers during production,
remain rigidly straight after separation.

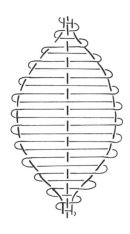

Above: a better machine-
made leaf. Though very
similar, it is not totally
identical to the hand-made
(see p.46).

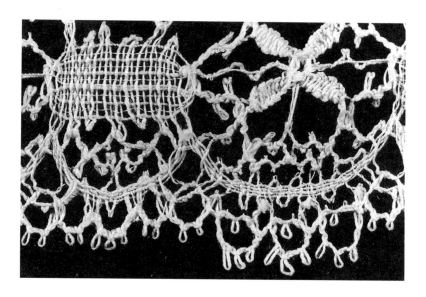

Left: hand-made Le Puy flounce.

Imitation by Leavers centre gimp (below) Two examples arranged as made.

Left: free edge scalloped, with picots. Threads pass straight down, not diagonally. Heavy yarns carried through the ground from one motif to the next or cut above and below.

Right: a flounce made widthwise of the machine. The short horizontal fining-throws show which way up the lace was made. Consecutive flounces have been separated by cutting across the border, in a scalloping manner.

DROSCHEL

Below: 'vrai' (true) droschel, the primary inspiration of machine nets, has 2 vertical sides plaited four times, the other 4 sides twisted. Copied at great expense, the best was said to cost more than the hand-made.

Above, and below left: hand-made Honiton motifs applied to a machine droschel net.

Below right: muslin attached by a cord, in the style of Carrickmacross, to an imitation droschel.

Though the resemblance is remarkable, the mesh sides are not properly plaited.

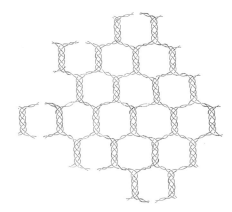

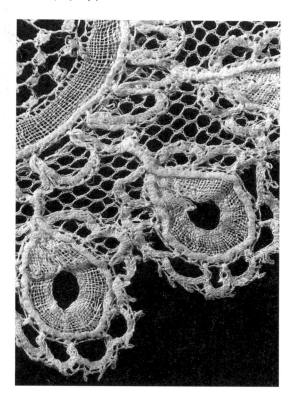

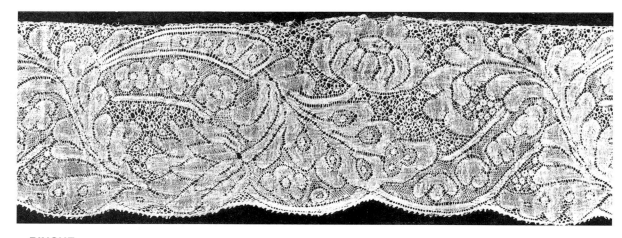

BINCHE

Continuous-thread bobbin lace, Flanders/Belgium, this example early 18th century, fine linen.
Solid areas: clothstitch or halfstitch, no gimp.
Meshwork: snowflakes.

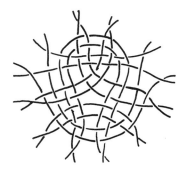

Above: detail of a snowflake.
Threads may turn vertically back
on themselves, but still continue
across the lace.

Imitation by Leavers bobbin fining (3 examples)
Right: c1890, arranged as made.

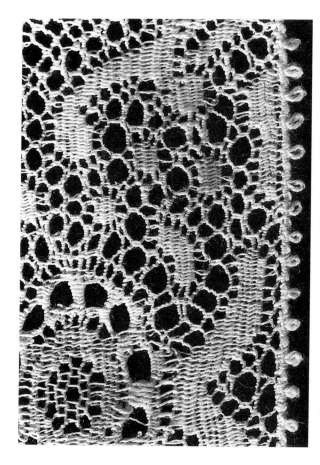

Above: c1910, arranged as worn.

Below: c1930, design in point de fée style.

Threads: general direction straight down, no vertical turning back, no diagonal passage. No clear continuity between picots and lace.
Horizontal throws short, zigzagging through the solid areas.

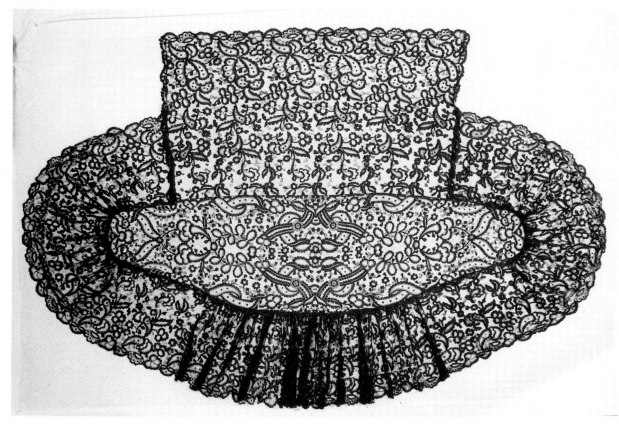

BLONDE
Spanish mantilla.
Continuous-thread bobbin lace, Spanish/French, mid-19th century, silk.
Solid areas: clothstitch and halfstitch, in heavy silk.
Gimp: clearly held by threads which pass across it.

Right: detail.

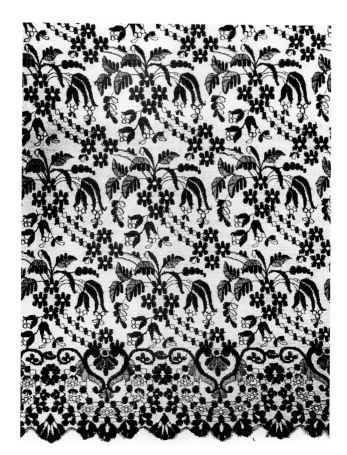

Imitation by Leavers centre gimp, bottom bar (i.e. with an additional set of beam threads) (left) Arranged as worn. Rayon.

Threads pass straight down, not diagonally. Cut above and below motifs. Although the design curves, the threads pass only lengthwise and widthwise.

No liners. Heavy threads carried across ground as floats, and cut on either side of solid areas, leaving small tufts.

Meshwork: Bishops net, with a cross at the top and bottom of each mesh. It looks like bobbinet, but the threads pass straight down, not diagonally (see p.31).

Repeats: short, vertically and horizontally.

Imitation by Lace Curtain (below)

Solid areas: two densities formed by top and bottom board spools.

Meshwork: Swiss ground (p.30).

Threads pass straight down, not diagonally. Scallops along lower border are cut, then finished with machine picots.

Imitation by Leavers centre gimp, bottom bar (above)
Solid areas: long widthwise throws of bronze rayon
yarn, some cut back above and below the motifs,
others pillaring through the net.
Meshwork: Bishops net in fine black yarn. Reverse
side, net continues through the solid areas.
Threads do not follow curvature of design but pass
straight down the lace.

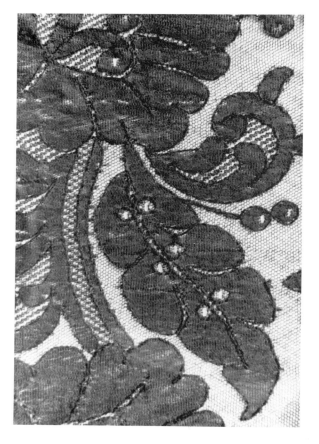

Imitation by Pusher (right)
Arranged as made.
All threads of equal thickness.
Solid, decorative areas and ground: bobbin threads
pass diagonally forming halfstitch clothwork and
halfstitch net.
Parallel striations (warp yarns) pass lengthwise.
Liners: run in with a sewing needle, mostly in
continuity, with cuts on one side only.

Imitation by run embroidery
a. Above: Run silk on warp-knitted net.
Solid areas: black silk run in and out of the meshes. Cuts
appear on one side only of each motif (note spots).

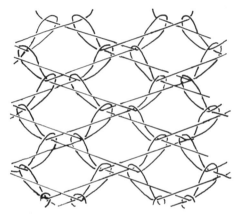

Right: detail of the net, reverse side.

b. Below: Run embroidery on 4-twist cotton net, using
two thicknesses of silk or cotton thread to give an
impression of clothstitch and halfstitch.

Right: detail.

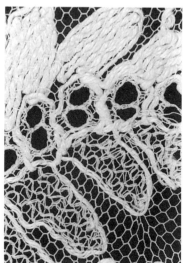

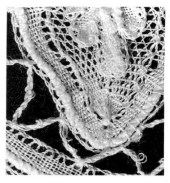

Right: snatch-pin ground.

Below: Schiffli detail.

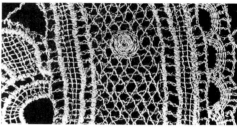

BRUGES/DUCHESSE
Above: choker collar of Bruges flower lace.
Non-continuous thread bobbin lace, Belgium, c1900. Cotton or linen.
Solid areas: mainly clothstitch. Design elements rather tape-like, running into each other. Decorative areas: bobbin lace fancy stitches. Guipure ground: plaited bars with picots arranged as large meshes attached by sewings, or plaited strands of snatch-pin fastened by needle and thread to the motifs.

Below: large collar of Brussels Duchesse.
As Bruges, except that design elements are neatly separated, and decorative areas include some needle fillings.

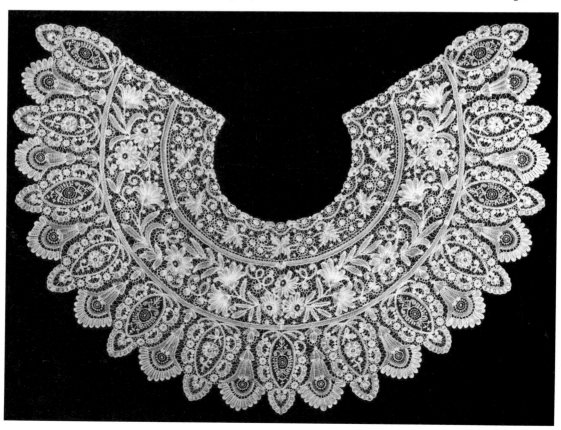

Imitation by Schiffli chemical lace (above)
Made entirely of lockstitch, following the curves of the
motifs. An impression of fuzziness.
No crossed or twisted threads, no buttonhole stitches.

Imitation by tambour embroidery (below)
Solid areas made by chain-stitching.
Picots: machine yardage stitched along cut edge of net.
Background: 4-twist net.

Imitation by Leavers bobbin fining (below)
Bruges design, with guipure ground.

BUCKS, LILLE, AND SIMILAR.

Continuous-thread bobbin laces, mainly England, France and Denmark, 19th to 20th centuries. Cotton, some linen. Above: Lille. Solid areas: clothstitch. Decorative areas: forms of honeycomb or tallies (see p.46). Ground: halfstitch meshwork. Gimp: cut on lower side only. Clear passage of threads in all areas.

Below: design for machine imitation by H.Marshall, Paris (courtesy: Birkin)

Imitation by Leavers independent
(right and below right)

Liners: cut above and below
motifs, not clearly held by threads
which pass across them.
Ground: all 6 sides of meshes
twisted, not crossed.
Picots: not clearly connected with
lace.
Tallies (spots) made by short
throws of patterning yarns.

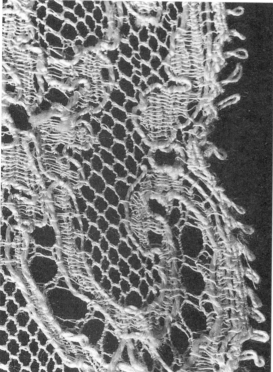

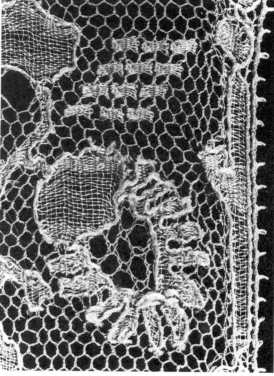

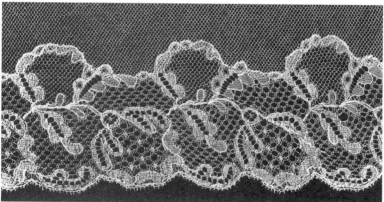

Imitation by Leavers bobbin fining
(left and above left)

Solid areas: bobbin fining with
zigzags. Ground: meshwork of
Ensor net. Liners: cut above and
below, crossed by short throws, no
diagonal passage. Course of
threads difficult to follow. The lace
is attached to bobbinet.

CHANTILLY

Above: huge Pusher shawl c1860s, fine mohair.
Pusher could make up to 6-foot square pieces, without joins.
Scalloped edges cut back by hand and tidied by attachment of machine picots.
Diagonal passage of threads in all areas, but warps appear as longitudinal ribbing, at right angles to the cross-ends of the meshes.

Imitation by run embroidery (left)
Ground: 2-twist silk bobbinet continuing throughout the lace.
Solid areas: run stitches passing in and out of the meshes, cuts on one side of motifs only.

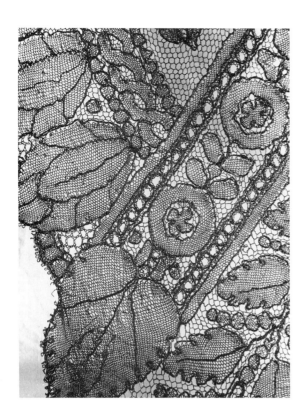

Left: detail of hand-made Chantilly

Continuous-thread bobbin lace, France, c1870s. Matt silk. Solid areas: halfstitch with straight threads passing widthwise as made, that is parallel to the cross-ends of the meshes (see p.16).
Meshwork: halfstitch ground.
Gimp: clearly clasped by threads passing between design and ground.
Note: large pieces are made in strips approximately 4-inch wide, but picots are still handmade, their threads continuous with the lace.

Imitation by warp knitting (below)

Solid areas: silk knitted loops run in vertical pillars on the face side. No crossed or twisted threads.
Ground: knitted loops connect sideways at frequent intervals.
Liner: run in by hand.
Machine picots separately attached.

Imitation by Pusher (above)
A 1920s rayon flounce, marketed as 'Chantilly'. Machine picots added. Technical details as p.60.

(below) Part of a Pusher fan leaf, c 1890, arranged as made (align by reference to crosses at top and bottom of each mesh) Liner: run in by hand, with the minimum of cuts. These may be on any side, as convenient for the 'runner', but never on both sides of the same motif.

Imitation by Leavers bobbin fining (above)
A flounce made crosswise of the machine, silk or rayon. Note cut threads along top and bottom, the scalloped border finished with attached machine picots. Solid areas: typical zigzags. No diagonal passage, threads pass straight down.
Liners: cut above and below each motif (see spots).

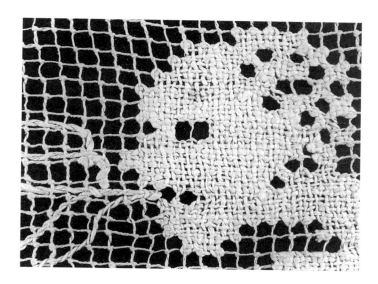

FILET/LACIS

Above: embroidered lace, Europe and the Far East, 16th to 20th centuries, linen or cotton.
Ground: hand-knotted square meshes. Direction of fishernet knots reversed in each row as fabric is turned (see p.36).
Solid areas: running- or darning-stitch in and out of the meshes.

Imitation by Leavers centre gimp (below)
Solid areas: effect of run stitch produced by long throws of the beam threads held in straight lines between bobbin and warp yarns. No movement in and out of meshes.
Scalloping: border cut away between the straight edges which are held by lacers.
Ground: no knots. Some pillaring.

Below: detail

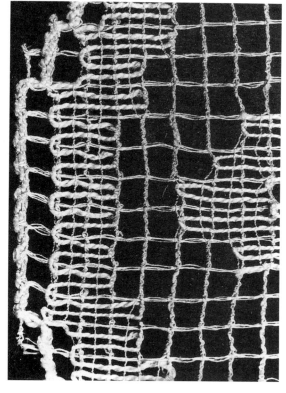

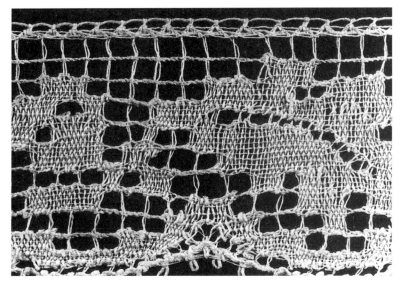

Imitation by Leavers independent (above)
Arranged as used. No knots. Meshwork: does not continue through the design.
Picots: usually absent in hand-made form. Path of threads unclear.

Imitation by Schiffli chemical lace (right and below)

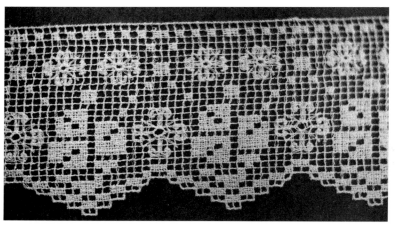

Two examples. No knots, but net appears to continue through the lace.
Good simulation of darning, but lockstitch fabric gives fuzzy effect.

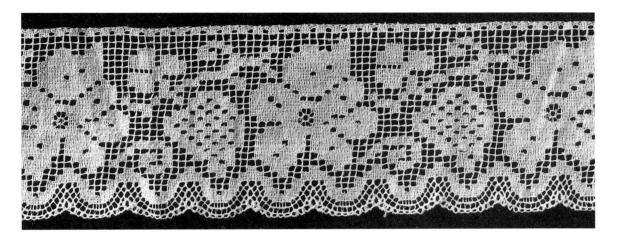

Imitation by Lace Curtain machine (above)
Net: no knots, but meshwork continues throughout the lace.
Pattern threads pillar in the ground.
Solid areas: Jacquard-controlled throws of spool threads produce 'run' effect, but yarns do not pass in and out of the meshes.
This Lace Curtain net was sometimes produced plain for hand embroidery.

Right: detail of filet net with spool-thread clothing.

All imitations cotton.

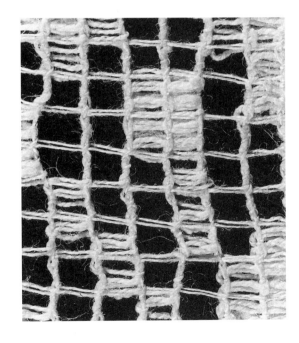

HONITON

Above: non-continuous thread bobbin lace, England, example mid-19th century. Cotton.
Solid areas: clothstitch and halfstitch. In the leaves and petals the threads turn back in a snake-like manner.
Gimp: a thin strand at the outer border of the motifs, cut on one side only.
Ground: guipure of plaited bars bearing small picots, attached to solid areas by sewings (alternatively by snatch-pin, needle-made meshes or leadworks).
Decorative fillings: groupings of leadworks attached by sewings, sometimes 3-dimensional raised work.
Design: diffuse, without repeats.
Looped picots along free edge.

Imitation by Leavers independent (below)
No turning back of threads, they lie straight down and uncurved. Rigidly repetitive design.

Imitation by Schiffli chemical lace
Two examples. All parts made by lockstitch. No sewings. Picots made by longer stitches, without looping. No crossing or twisting of threads. Embroidery can follow curvature of design.

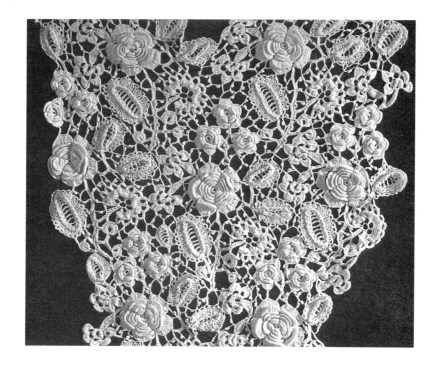

IRISH CROCHET
Above: Ireland, c1900, cotton or linen. Every part made of fine chain-stitch worked with a crochet hook.

Imitation by Schiffli chemical lace (below)

Imitation by Schiffli chemical lace (left)
Every part made of lockstitch, but simulation of reality
enhanced by the sewing on of hand-crocheted roses with
raised petals.

Right: detail of imitation crochet-
type ground. The circles, and the
opening between the crossed
stalks, were created by borers
piercing the degradable cloth
during manufacture, then sewn
around with blatt stitch. The
raised ovals were made by
repeated oversewing.

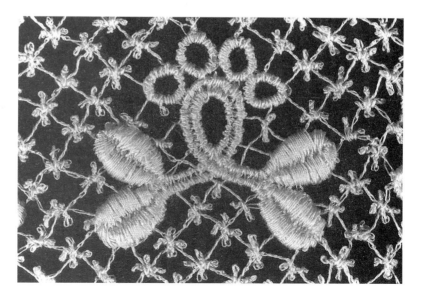

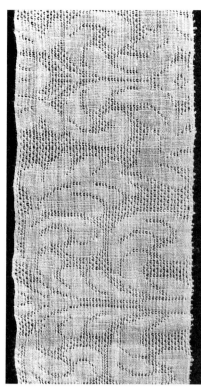

LOOM LACES

Left: woven lace, German, 19th century, made on a hand loom (see p.23). Standing and crossing warps twine around each weft pick, their various manoevres making a design.

Imitation by Leavers bobbin fining (right)
Straight-down thread passage, the path difficult to follow. Picots rigidly lined up. Zigzagging in solid areas. No twining of warps.

— x — x — x —

MALTESE

Below: continuous-thread bobbin lace, Gozo and Malta, c1910. Silk. Solid areas: clothstitch. No gimp. Ground: compact guipure of plaited strands intermixed with fat leaves. Picots: plaited loops.

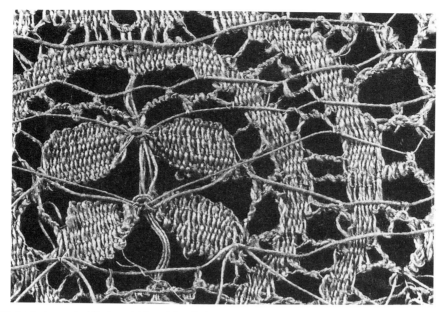

Imitation by Leavers independent (below right and detail above)
Auxiliary threads used to support picots on bars. Apparent curvature of threads an illusion. Picots: made over a rigid lacer.

Imitation by Leavers centre gimp (below left)
Threads pass straight down, not diagonally, their course difficult to follow.

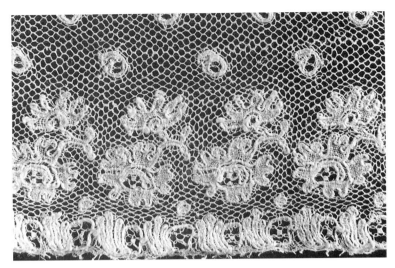
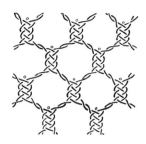

MECHLIN

Above: continuous-thread bobbin lace, Belgium, this example second half 19th century. Cotton.

Solid areas: clothstitch.

Gimp: silky effect, appears equally on both sides of the lace.

Picots: small loops along the heading.

Ground: network of hexagonal meshes, the vertical sides plaited three times, the remaining sides twisted (detail above right).

Repeats: short, with slight differences between them.

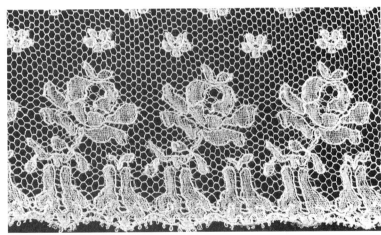

Imitation by Leavers independent (above)

Threads pass straight down, not diagonally.

Ground: with magnification seen to be not clearly plaited.

Liner: unevenly enclosed by threads passing across it. Cut above and below each motif.

Repeats: Jacquard-controlled and identical.

Imitation by Leavers bobbin fining (right)

Solid areas not 'woven' but appear as zigzags.

Ground: vertical 'plaits' like two threads needleweaving around two others, the 'twisted' sides not at all clear.

Imitation by run embroidery on net (Isle of Wight lace).

Not illustrated.

Left: Mechlin bobbin-made, c1870. Arranged as made. Cotton.
Gimp: unusual - prominent on face side, flat on the reverse, neatly held by threads entering and leaving the motifs. It frequently turns back on itself and is cut on lower side only.
Other features as on p.72, but a vertical streakiness caused by irregular spinning of thread gives a straight-down look and this, combined with the unusually thick gimp, or liner, the use of cotton yarn and the imitation of an 18th-century design, make it appear at first sight machine-made.

Right: two forms of 'Mechlin' net made on special Warp Looms using warp threads only.

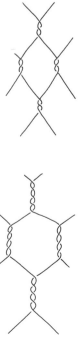

MILANESE

Above: non-continuous thread bobbin lace, Italy, this example c1700. Linen.
Solid areas: clothstitch in the form of shaped tapes often pierced with decorative openings, the threads curving to follow the shape of the design (see p.75, below).
Fancy stitches numerous, all made from cross and twist sequences. Ground: guipure of thin bars attached by sewings.

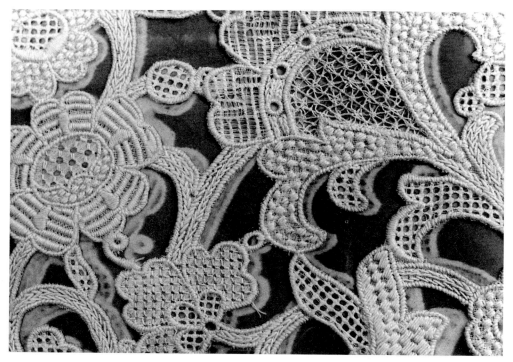

Imitation by Handmachine chemical lace (above)
The rows of stitches can curve to follow the shapes of the design, but there are no crosses or twists, no sewings, and the original cloth remains within the petals.

Opposite, below: *Imitation by cloth appliqué* onto a variety of Leavers fancy nets. These are trimmed back on the reverse side to look like fillings.
Ground: handmade bars of twisted threads.
Liner: a couched cord, not typical of the original.
No curvature of threads to follow the shapes. No sewings.

Below: detail of Milanese bobbin lace showing curvature of threads and, here, plaited bars.

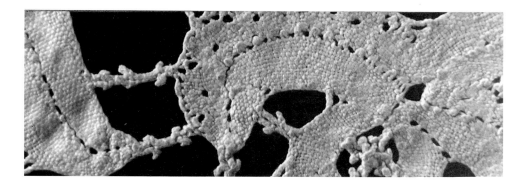

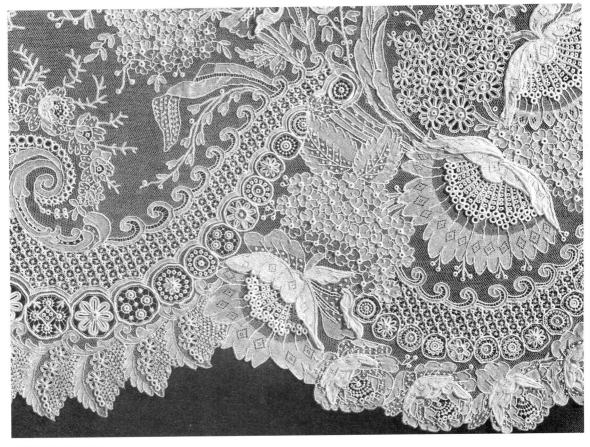

POINT DE GAZE

Above: needle lace, Belgium, this example late 19th century. Cotton.

Solid areas: detached buttonhole stitches with a straight return, the lines of stitches following the curves of scrolls, petals and leaves.

Decorative areas: all various types or arrangements of buttonhole-stitch. The flowers have raised petals separately attached.

Cordonnet: strands of thread held by spaced buttonhole stitching.
Ground: detached buttonhole stitches in every row.

Detail: p. 77.

Imitation by Singer sewing machine (left)
Instructions for making this lace appeared in 1911. No degradable fabric was used. Every minute space was cut away by hand before being filled with imitation needle-lace stitches, using lockstitch.

76

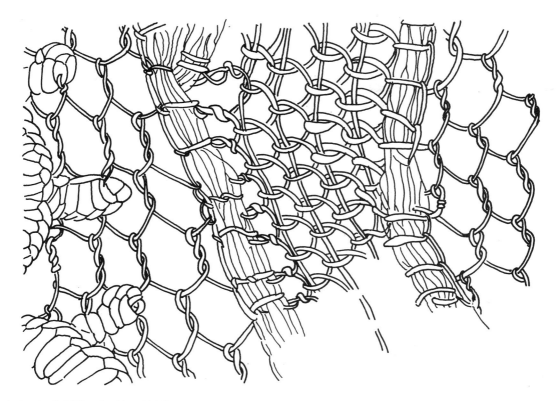

Imitation by Schiffli embroidery (right)
Solid areas: entirely lockstitch embroidery on 2-twist bobbinet.
No buttonhole stitches. Decorative spaces created by cutting
net away on reverse side, not by a chemical process. Small
whiskers of thread remain. Raised petals are of cut cloth,
bordered with blatt-stitch, and attached by hand or by a single-
needle lockstitch sewing machine.

Imitation by Schiffli chemical lace (below)
Embroidery on a degradable fabric, later removed, leaving a
mixture of guipure and net-like grounds. All lockstitch.

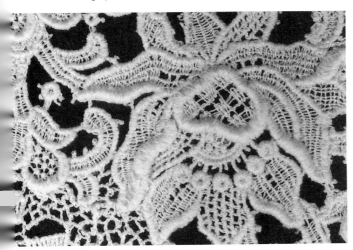

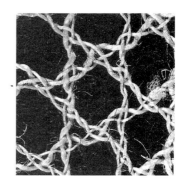

POINT DE PARIS

Left: Continuous-thread bobbin lace, France, early 20th century. Cotton.
Solid areas: clothstitch.
Gimp: single cut on lower side.
Ground: six-point star meshwork (detail above).
Footing: exchange bobbins.
Threads pass diagonally.

Imitation by Leavers independent
Right: This is a direct copy of the bobbin-made sample. (From a Birkin booklet containing four hand and four machine laces of matched design, and the text: 'BB laces. Wonderful reproductions shown side by side with the original Hand Made Goods. Can you tell the difference?').

Below: detail of net ground.

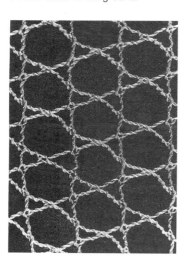

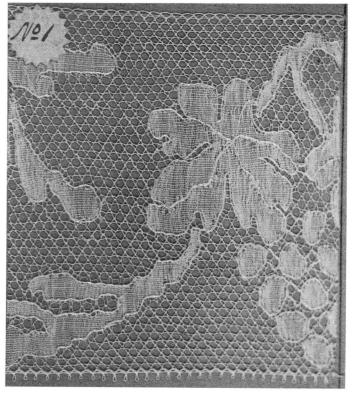

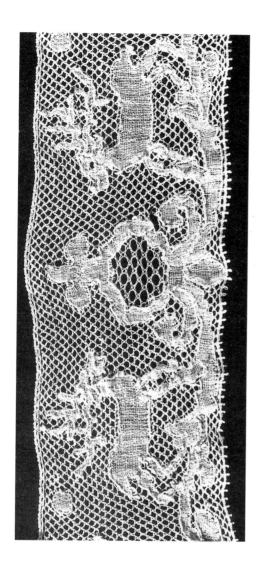

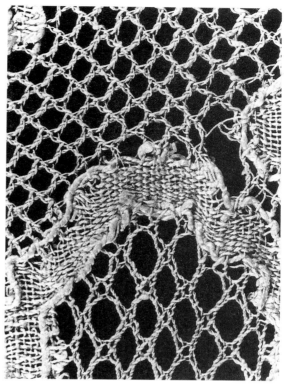

Leavers independent. (see p. 78)
Threads pass straight down, not diagonally. Straight 'gathering' threads run along the footing, no exchange bobbins. Liners have cuts above and below and are crossed by irregular threads. Passage of threads between picots and lace not clear.

Left, and detail above: a pair of stags, arranged as made.

Below right: detail of a different form of Leavers point de Paris ground. The threads appear to run diagonally but in fact only go back and forth between one vertical line and the next. Grounds of this type are sometimes used for run or tambour embroidery.

Imitation by warp knitting (below) Early 19th century.
Used as a base for hand-embroidery.

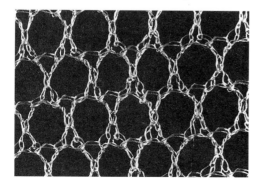

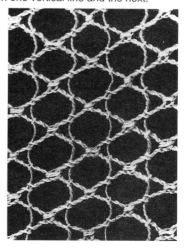

RESEAU VENISE
Above: needle lace, Italy, mid-18th century. Fine hand-spun linen.

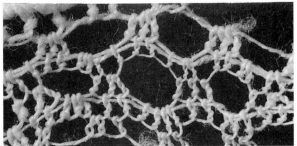

Solid areas: detached buttonhole stitch with a straight return (up to 10,000 stitches per square inch).
Decorative fillings: numerous, all variations of buttonhole stitching (detail left).
Ground: meshwork of twisted buttonhole stitch with whipped return.
Totally flat, no cordonnet or other raised work.

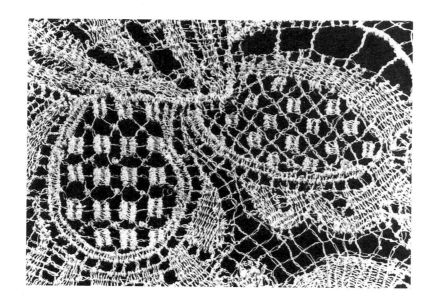

Imitation by Schiffli
Above and below left: chemical guipure with sparse meshwork.

Below right: embroidery on bobbinet.
Both of fuzzy-looking lockstitch, no buttonhole stitching.

RETICELLA/CUTWORK

Cutwork (above): an embroidered lace, Italy and throughout Europe, 17th century. Linen.
Squares cut out of woven fabric, fragments of which are left where residual warps and wefts cross. Elsewhere frames strengthened with overcasting or needleweaving. Decorative triangles outlined with a laid cord and filled with close detached buttonhole stitches.

Reticella (left): needle lace, 19th-century copy of 17th-century original. No woven cloth. Square frames made of plaited strands knotted together where they intersect.

Neither has a structured ground. Design and openwork form a unity. Linen.

Imitation by Schiffli chemical lace
Above and below left: all lockstitch. No buttonhole stitches, no plaiting, no needleweaving. Cotton.

Imitation by Handmachine chemical lace
Below: solid areas appear darned. No buttonhole stitches, though a few may be added by hand. Simulated needleweaving along the frames. Cotton.

ROSALINE
Above: Non-continuous thread bobbin lace, Belgium, late 19th century. Cotton.
Solid areas: clothstitch and halfstitch, bordered with small loop picots.
Flower centres decorated with raised needle-made circles. Ground: guipure of thin strands passing through edges of motifs, linking them together.

Imitation by Schiffli chemical lace (below)
Lockstitch only, the raised circles created by repeated oversewing sometimes over long base stitches which act as padding. Bordering picots made of extended stitches. Bars: jump stitch. Cotton.

RUSSIAN

Above: Bobbin lace of sinuous worm-like form, narrower spaces crossed by continuous threads, meshes of wider areas attached by sewings. This example bought in Archangel in 1899. Silk.
Solid areas: clothstitch with threads following the curvature.

Imitation by Leavers independent (left)
Straight-down passage of threads obscured by apparent turning back, but cut ends at top and bottom of evey curve reveal the general downward direction of manufacture. Silk.

Imitation by Schiffli chemical lace (below)
Lockstitch only. Movements of frame allow lines of stitches to curve freely. Repeats regular and precise. Cotton.

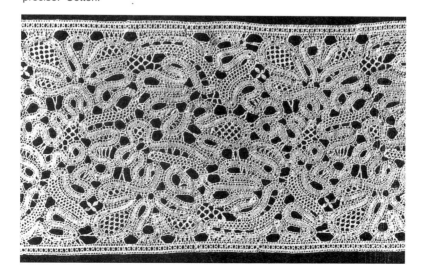

TAPE-BASED LACES
Above: Craft lace, made throughout Europe, often domestic. This example mid-19th century. Linen or cotton.
Solid areas: Straight machine (or bobbin-made) tapes or braids gathered or folded as required to fit outline of design.
Decorative fillings: varied needle lace stitches.
Ground: needle-made. Variable, sometimes a meshwork, here a guipure of buttonholed bars with picots.

Imitation by Leavers bobbin fining (below)
No separate tapes, no buttonhole stitches, no folding or gathering.

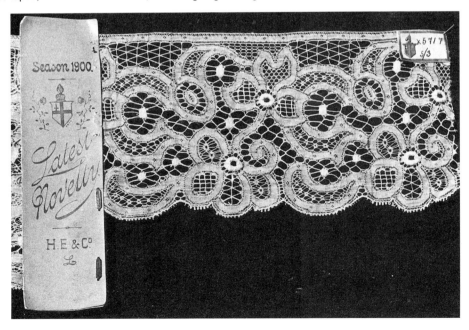

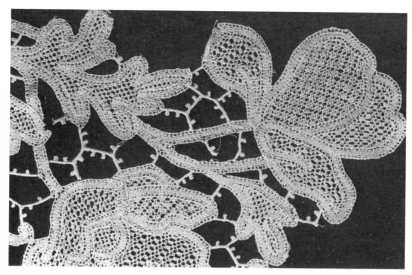

Imitation by Schiffli chemical lace (above)
All lockstitch, and made in one, not as distinct tapes and fillings.

Imitation by Leavers independent (below, arranged as made).
As for bobbin fining, except that the 'tapes' appear woven, not zigzagged. Ground of Ensor net. Pillaring.

Below: *Bobbin fining* imitating fancy tapes of a kind produced for the domestic embroiderer.

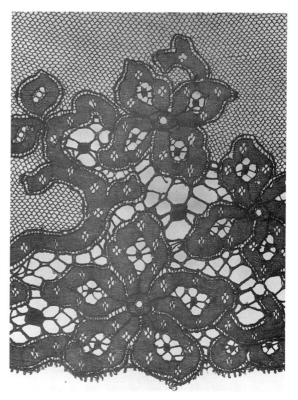

TENERIFFE/SUN LACE/WHEEL LACE

Left: craft lace made with a needle. Paraguay, Mexico or Canary Islands, 19th to 20th centuries. Silk, sometimes fine cotton.
Solid areas: cut-out or outlined circles crossed by numerous diameters with design woven in and out using a sewing needle.

Imitation by Singer sewing machine.
'The Singer Instructions for Art Embroidery', published in 1911, describes how to make Teneriffe wheels using a single-needle domestic sewing machine (not illustrated).

Imitation by Leavers independent. Cotton.
Below left: threads pass straight down, not in a circular direction. Lace made as a whole, not as separate pieces. No needle-weaving, solid areas look plain-woven. Cotton.

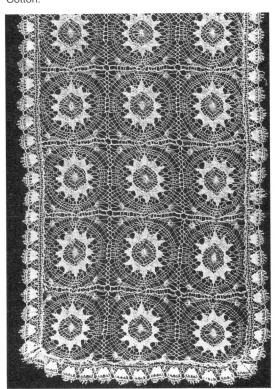

Below: detail of hand-made Teneriffe.

TORCHON and YAK

Left: Continuous-thread bobbin lace, made throughout Europe, 19th to 20th centuries. Linen or cotton. Below: Yak, wool.
Solid areas: clothstitch and/or halfstitch.
Decorative features: spiders and fans. Yak, often whorls of leaves like the spokes of a wheel.
Ground: torchon mesh. Yak, 5-hole.
Picots: twisted threads extending from the fans. Yak, plaited points.

Imitation by Barmen (below, arranged as made)

2-thread example with lengthwise-running pillar threads in footing and elsewhere. Moving threads follow diagonal passage.
Halfstitch: straight threads run lengthwise.
Picots: made over a rigid lacer, they keep their straight line-up after it has been removed.
Ground: torchon stitch. Linen or cotton.

Below: plaits too tightly twisted. Diagonal clothstitch.

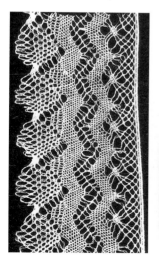

Detail: pillars along the footside. Diagonal halfstitch. Compare spiders with hand-made, above.

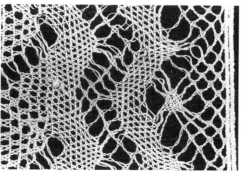

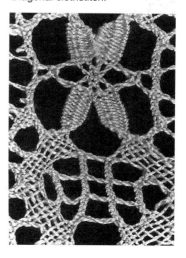

Imitation by Leavers centre gimp (shown above with
detail below left).
Threads pass straight down or briefly sideways.
Halfstitch appearance: throws of warp threads across the
longitudinal bobbin threads, the two sets tied by beam
threads.
Footing: straight lengthwise 'gathering' threads, no
exchange bobbins.
Spiders and leaves: clumsily made. Cotton.

Below right: *Leavers hybrid*, a combination of traversed
net and straight-down pattern areas with long throws.

Above: typical Barmen footing. No
exchange bobbins.

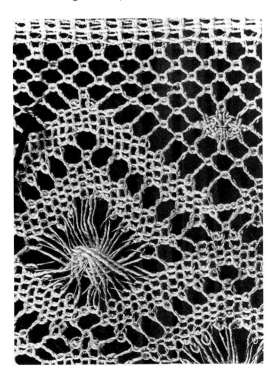

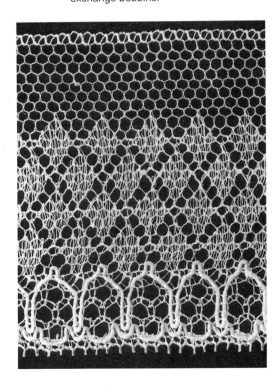

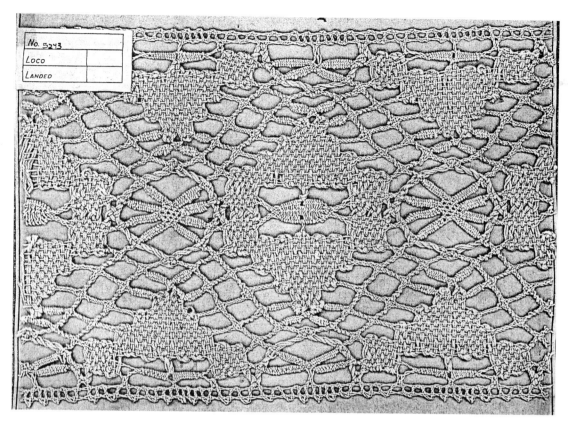

No. 5243
Loco
Landed

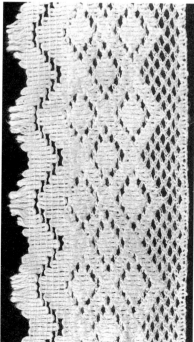

Imitation by 1-thread Barmen
(above)
Footside, picots and plainweave clothstitch well simulated, but no exchange bobbins, and plaits and leaves too tight. Cotton. (Courtesy: Birkin, Nottingham)

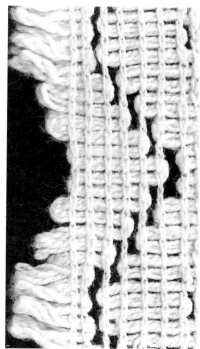

Imitation by Warp Frame/Raschel
(left, and detail right)
This example early 20th century. Cotton.
No diagonal passage, threads run straight down. Solid areas made by inlay yarns passing widthwise and held by vertical pillars of knitted loops. Angularity of lines of picots indicates use of lacers.

VALENCIENNES

Continuous-thread bobbin lace, France, this example c1910. Cotton. Solid areas: clothstitch. No gimp. Border of small holes around motifs, formed by extra twists. Ground: square (diamond-shaped) plaited meshes.

Imitation by Leavers bobbin fining Solid areas: zigzags. Ground: not true plaiting. Note distortion of meshes at the right-hand side. Cotton.

Detail of hand-made lace.

Detail of machine lace.

Both arranged as made.

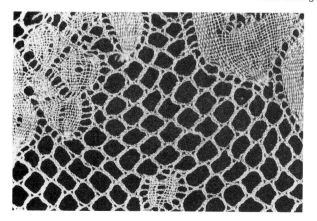

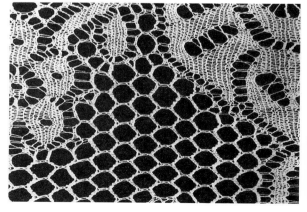

Imitation by Leavers independent
Solid areas: dense and extensive 'clothstitch'. Excess threads cut back above and below motifs
(detail below right).
Course of threads in ground difficult to follow,
especially in 'plaits'.
Picots not clearly connected to the lace.
Footing not typical of bobbin laces.

Below: detail of imitation plaited ground
and simulated thread curvature, in
another example.

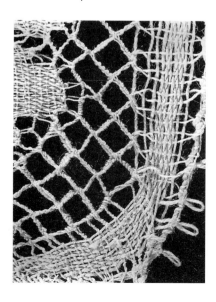

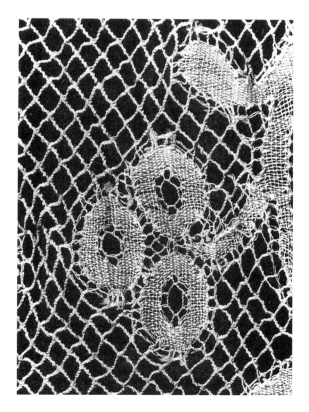

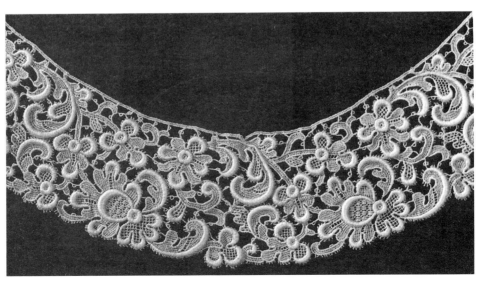

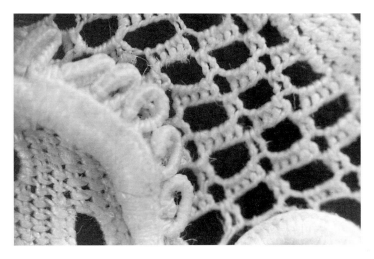

VENETIAN LACE, RAISED AND FLAT

P.94 top, and detail left: needle lace, Italy, second half 17th century. Linen.

Solid areas: detached buttonhole stitch with a straight return.

Decorative fillings: various types and arrangements of buttonhole stitch.

Cordonnet: heavily padded, closely covered with buttonhole stitching, frequently extended into picots.

Ground: short bars buttonholed over, and decorated.

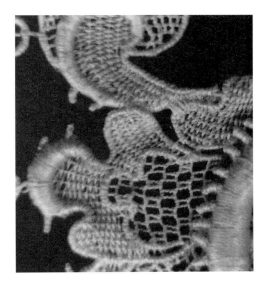

Imitation by Handmachine (p.94 middle, and detail left)
Solid areas: appear darned. No buttonhole stitching.
Fillings: simulated buttonhole stitches, occasionally finished by hand.
Raised outlines: formed by repeated oversewing. Cotton.

Imitation by Schiffli (p.94 below, and detail right)
Entirely lockstitch, no buttonhole stitches.
Raised work: formed by repeated oversewing.
Cotton.

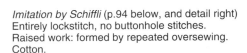

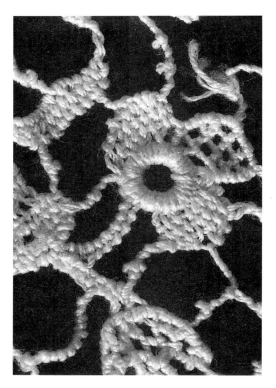

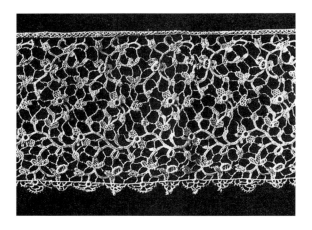

Imitation of Venetian coralline by Handmachine chemical lace (above and left)
Note regular repeat, indicating automated patterning.

Below left: imitation by *Handmachine chemical lace* (openwork) and surface embroidery on cloth (solid areas).

Imitation by Leavers centre gimp (below)
No buttonhole stitches in solid areas or ground, but raised liner buttonholed over and couched down by hand. Pillaring along bars. Ensor net as fillings. Cotton.

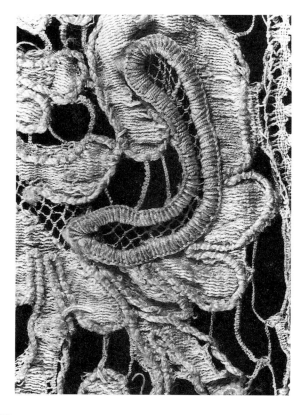